CW00741724

GET UNSTUCK

Ditch your Drama and Move from Pain to Power

Niamh Sheeran Ennis

Get Unstuck

Copyright © Niamh Sheeran Ennis 2022

All rights reserved. No part of this book may be reproduced or utilised in any form or by any means, electronic or mechanical, including photocopying, recording or by any information storage and retrieval system, without permission in writing from Book Hub Publishing.

The information presented is the author's opinion and does not constitute professional health or medical advice. The content of this book is for informational purposes only and is not intended to diagnose, treat, cure, or prevent any condition or disease.

The author and publisher are providing this book and its contents on an "as is" basis and make no representations or warranties of any kind with respect to this book or its contents. The author and publisher disclaim all such representations and warranties including, for example, warranties of merchantability and healthcare for a particular purpose.

In addition, the author and publisher do not represent or warrant that the information accessible via this book is entirely accurate, complete or current. Please consult with your own physician or healthcare specialist regarding the suggestions and recommendations made in this book.

Except as specifically stated in this book, neither the author or publisher will be liable for damages arising out of or in connection with the use of this book. This is a comprehensive limitation of liability that applies to all damages of any kind, including (without limitation) compensatory; direct, indirect or consequential damages; loss of data, income or profit; loss of or damage to property and claims of third parties.

Before you begin any healthcare programme, or change your lifestyle in any way, you are advised to consult your physician or another licensed healthcare practitioner to ensure that you are in good health and that the examples/advice contained in this book will not harm you.

This book provides content related to physical and/or mental health issues. As such, use of this book implies your acceptance of this disclaimer.

The views expressed in this book are the author's and not necessarily those of the publisher. We are happy to rectify any mistakes/omissions/errors should these be pointed out to us.

Published by Book Hub Publishing, An Independent Publishing House, Galway and Limerick, Ireland. www.bookhubpublishing.com

*Book Hub Publishing uses paper sourced from sustainable forestry. We are committed to inclusion and diversity.

"I absolutely love Niamh Ennis! With grit, grace and good humour, Niamh will guide you to get clear on the life you really want to live and support you to step into it today. Release the pain of the past and free yourself from living the same story.

Get Unstuck is a brilliant book that will inspire you to embrace change and turn your challenges into the opportunities for transformation."

—*Rebecca Campbell, bestselling author.*

This is a book for people who want help, support and most importantly, results. Niamh's style of coaching is personal and personable, delivered with empathy, humour and above all, great wisdom. I make no big decisions in life without consulting Niamh.

She has a canny skill for clarity and getting right to the point. If you want more from life, I can't think of a better way to start than with this book, and with Niamh on your side.

—*Melanie Morris, Director & Contributing Editor, IMAGE Media*

I've been lucky to know Niamh for a few years now and I am always in awe of her warmth and wisdom. She's someone that walks her talk and Get Unstuck is not only an intimate memoir that reminds us we aren't alone, but also, a practical guide to moving on from setbacks – even the big ones that knock us over. Thank you, Niamh, for sharing your heart with us.

—*Lucy Sheridan, The Comparison Coach*

For David Sheeran, my Dad

My father didn't tell me how to live; he lived and let me watch him do it.

—Clarence Budington Kelland

THANK YOUS

I have so much to be thankful for and so many individuals to say it to. I always thought that writing the acknowledgements would be the easiest part of this process. As a child I daydreamed about who I'd mention, but now it's here, I'm simply terrified that I'll forget someone! So many people inspired me on this journey and lots more came into my life and pushed and prodded me along the way. Too many to mention by name but they absolutely know who they are.

To my publishers Susan and Niall at BookHub Publishing. You helped me make this book a physical reality and the fact that we signed our deal on 22.02.2022 was all the proof I needed that we would do it with the full support of the Universe! I'm deeply grateful for your wisdom, patience, support and kindness.

To Rebecca Campbell for inspiring me to write this book. I always knew it would happen but I could not see how, until I read your first book and everything changed inside me. The fact that you agreed to write the cover endorsement really felt like a full circle moment.

To Melanie Morris for your friendship and cheerleading skills when writing this book and for distracting me with copious reality-television voice notes along the way. To Lucy Sheridan, mentor and all-round wonderfully wise woman and expressor of very kind words.

To Lauren Burles, Elaine O'Neill, Jessica Killingley, Roisin Meaney, Elizabeth McCrory, Colm O'Comartun, Ray Flannery and Cormac Kinsella for all of your valuable guidance and support.

Behind every woman is another strong woman and I've benefited from having the very best in my life - Caitriona Fottrell, Caroline Kennedy, Louise McNally, Siobhan Kelly, Ciara Holmes, Ann Harper, Mary Moorhead, Dee Shalloe, Edel O'Malley and Paula Comerford. These friendships have been one of my life's blessings. And to my family, old and new, the Keenans and the Ennis'.

To my husband Michael, for being patient with my long absences while writing this, for keeping our dog entertained at the weekends and for creating the perfect environment where it felt safe for me to share all parts of this story. I love and am grateful for you.

I'm guessing few dogs get mentioned by name, but my loyal companion, Bella is the exception. Walking through the woods, each and every morning, she tolerated me stopping and randomly asking the trees for their words of wisdom, which always came.

To you reading this. Thank you, from my heart to yours, for picking up this book. My intention always was that this would serve to inspire and activate in you a belief that change is not just possible but that it is entirely possible for you; and that when you are fully ready, you will know exactly how to get unstuck.

Finally, I honour all of those incredible women who have permitted me to share their stories with you. Change isn't always the easiest option but it is always the best, and these stories bear witness to the power of change that exists inside each of you, when you are ready. Get Unstuck is for anyone looking for their way back.

With deep gratitude, Niamh x

CONTENTS PAGE

COME HOME

You can't move on while clinging to your past.

You can't learn to love yourself more until you agree to stop hating yourself less.

You can't heal from the hurt until you accept you didn't cause it.

You can't ask for help until you are willing to receive it.

It is in moments of surrender we learn our greatest lessons.

When you stop looking to others for your next steps, you discover the answers.

When you surrender to what might be, everything becomes possible.

The woman you have been searching for everywhere, all of these years, is right there inside of you, where she has been all along.

That part of you that you can hear whispering in the still of the night, calling to you is your soul.

Listen to it and allow it to take you to a place of surrender.

Let the walls down and the light in.

Begin making your way home.

—Niamh Ennis

INTRODUCTION

———————

Life-changing events are like Ronseal, they do exactly what they say on the tin. They change everything about who you are, how you cope and what you want. They disrupt who you were and how you were living. Life gets split into 'before' and 'after', into pre-event and post-event, and chaos reigns.

If you're standing somewhere between the two, the before and the after, in the middle of the madness, wondering what happened, then this book is for you.

If you're feeling lost, heartbroken, scared, worried, lacking purpose or wanting your share in life's sparkle, you will find some answers here.

If you find that nothing motivates you, you feel flat, irritated by everyone and need a proverbial kick in the rear, you'll find that here.

If you want to live a life that feels a lot more 'yours' and a lot less 'theirs', you'll discover just how, here.

If you've experienced loss of any kind, loss of loved ones,

loss of a relationship, loss of your future, loss of identity, loss of security, know that I have been where you are, and it is my desire now to guide you through the debris. I identify with how you are feeling and I know what helped me, and I write this in the hope that it could help you too. In each part of this book, I will stretch you and move you to places that may not always feel so familiar or comfortable.

This is what makes my work as a Transformation Coach a little unique and a lot special; I will challenge you, push you, hold you accountable and use the skills that life's experiences have given me, through every part of this process. But in each part and in every step, I promise that you will always feel heard and supported. I will share with you what my experience and that of my clients' has been and hope that you can resonate with some of it, so that it may serve you to grow and heal. I will keep *you* at the heart of everything.

I believe that your mindset informs all that you think you are and ultimately all that you do, but you may also need some practical next steps and a roadmap to keep you focused and provide reassurance that you are preparing to take the very next best step for you.

Every time you feel resistance rising, please know that I've been right where you are and that I know for sure how tough this is. I know it feels like the world is against you, I know you may well be angry that what's happened has happened. I honestly know all this. I can still recall every detail of that pain and loneliness I felt when I was at my lowest. That feeling never leaves you.

When you experience any life-changing event or personal setback – such as loss, death, illness, heartbreak, redundancy, financial troubles, family fallout, ending of friendships and relationships – something changes for you, which means something changes *in* you.

This book has been written to make you stop, to reflect and observe your actions and behaviour, and to do it from a place of compassion. Please don't be fooled into thinking that my stretching you and moving you to somewhere unfamiliar means that this read will feel hard and unpalatable. It won't, but it will require you to be extremely truthful and brutally honest with yourself. I want this book to encourage you to go inwards.

It's one thing to survive a life-changing event, but another to come out the other side. Many of us get stuck in the 'in-between'. What's that, you may ask? Well, it's that place where you have begun to define yourself by your experiences. You've turned a lesson into a life sentence. You've become the woman who...(fill in your blank). This horrendous thing happened in your life and, quite rightly, you were supported by others to help you overcome the pain. Only now, years later, you are still attached to their sympathy. You are stuck there.

You have allowed your story to become that of the event, and instead of overcoming it, you continue to live with it, day to day. You've become disconnected and blocked off those parts of you that help you to love and be lovable because it felt like a much better way to protect yourself from future hurt and disappointment. You feel unmotivated, uninspired, and are just about surviving. You may have even become addicted to the drama of it all, the woman who (fill in your blank) is your identity now. It's who you are and you're so comfortable in the misery of that story that you haven't even considered rewriting it.

A small part of you might want to, but the truth is you can't. You don't know how. What needs to happen is for you to detach yourself from this and move into the next part of your life, which is this one, here and now. This is the exact space where you will give yourself the permission to have faith to behave differently, to do something new so you can become someone else; to become the better and fuller version of yourself.

We crave moving past our feelings of pain, beyond the disappointment, loss and hurt. But to start doing this, we must admit that we have disconnected internally. Our heads – the part of us that thinks, plans, controls and manages everything – are no longer connected to our hearts – the place where our feelings, emotions, intuition, creativity and spirituality reside. This is a natural outcome when we experience shock or disappointment in life, but it's one that needs rectifying.

I've had to do all of this and because I know it to be true, I can see it in others. I see it in you. I want to encourage you to see it in yourself. I want this book to be that prompt and, in doing so, give you that push and the permission you are searching for – to reconnect and move yourself from pain to power. I want you to trust that this is possible. Because it is.

WHAT DID I NEED TO HEAR 10 YEARS AGO?

I needed to hear that the answers were within me, if I would only let myself listen. I yearned to see a way out of feeling so helpless and alone. I wish someone had simply been there to give me the 'not so gentle' nudge that would have inspired me to want to do more for myself.

But back then, I had no idea what was happening to me. I

didn't have the explanatory language and I most certainly didn't have the awareness. I craved a roadmap or at least an understanding of what was really going on inside me, what I could expect to feel next and a strategy for how to navigate my way entirely through it. Things had not gone according to plan; my life had imploded, and I wasn't coping well.

What happened to me happens to everyone, please believe me that I really do know that. But what made this a little unique was that many of these things happened at the same time. Whether you're grieving a death, or a loss, or the ending of a relationship, you absolutely need to grieve for as long as it takes. Take no shortcuts on this piece of work. However, you do not want to feel like a victim for any longer than you need to. Sympathy can be addictive, among many other things. Your past can easily define you, but it's you who gets to decide if it's going to determine your future as well.

I wrote my first book in 2018. At the time, it was the book I needed to write but nobody needed to read. And nobody did; it never saw the light of day. I see now that, at best, it was a purging exercise; and at worst, it was a lesson in self-indulgence! This book is different. I feel this and I know you will too.

What you need to hear about, which I'm assuming you do if you're reading this book, is how I transformed my own life. What changes I made, what worked for me and what didn't, the mistakes I made and the shortcuts I could recommend. I wasn't in a position to share any of this back then, because I still didn't know for sure. It was still all too raw.

That's the thing about the timing of what you share and what you teach. If the wound is still open, you are simply not ready. You're neither ready to teach or learn. But nor do you need to wait until your healing journey is complete, because, well, nobody would ever get to write or indeed read a book at that rate, knowing that this process has no ending. When you decide to heal, change or transform, you are in fact committing yourself to a lifelong process. Not always a linear one and not without its own challenges, it's one that is most certainly located well outside of your comfort zone; but the rewards are everything you imagine they might be and much, much more.

USING THIS BOOK

To begin, I'm going to share my own story with you, so that we can break the ice and help you understand me better. Then we are going to focus in on you. We'll dive into your story, explore where you might have become disconnected, so that we can observe just what is holding you back, before deciding on how to remove these blocks.

In the second part of this book, we will move you to that place where you will feel free and ready to give yourself the permission to heal, to restore your confidence, to rewrite your story so that you'll know again how it feels to be fully, positively and, dare I say it, authentically yourself. Fasten your seatbelts, it will most definitely be a bumpy ride!

It's important you understand that for this to work, for it to have the desired impact of helping you embrace change, you are going to need to show up and be prepared do the work! I can't do it for you, nor should you want me to, but if we work on this together, we can achieve great things!

I need to say this from the outset – this is not a book about grief. It is a guide on overcoming any of life's challenges or those unwanted life-changing events. Yes, grief plays a big part in my personal life-story, but my only intention here is to share all of the tools, steps and modalities that I have seen help people, when they are transforming their own life and learning how to become unstuck and start over again.

See which tools appeal to you, which do you like most, which are you curious about and then, over time, slowly start to implement them at a pace that feels right for you. Consider and absorb the thoughts, beliefs and ideas that are within these pages, and you will be drawn to what lands best with you. Trust that little voice inside, whispering gentle nudges on which direction to move.

In this book, I invite you to learn from the personal experiences I reveal, to be inspired by the (amended for ethical reasons) client conversations I share with you, all in the hope that you will feel less alone.

As you read each page, observe what resonates with you, what's inspiring you, what you feel is speaking directly to you. When you close your eyes, what can you imagine yourself changing? How will the transformation that will inevitably take place make you feel?

The stages of this book involve disconnecting and reconnecting, identifying your old story and rewriting your future one, detaching from your own drama and moving you from pain to power. So, you're going to need plenty of time, lots of headspace and a brand spanking new journal as well!

I will walk one short step behind you, offering tools and sharing client conversations along with mindset exercises that I encourage you to complete as you go through this process. Some of these are presented in a way so that you can assimilate these learnings into your everyday life, opening up a new way of thinking and being.

Use all of the stories you can access to inspire you, but know that you will only ever be able to find what you want when you finally accept it is inside of you. When we learn to recognise the difference between being inspired by others and imitating them, that's when we embody freedom. It begins when you stop seeing 'you' in others. It is here that your power lives: the power to be yourself. I want this for you. But you have to want it more.

Disclaimer: This book is not for the walking wounded. Pain needs to be felt before it can fully transform your life. So if you have just had your world come crashing down, please sit with it. Give yourself the space to breathe, to break if you need to. This book will be here for you when you are ready to rebuild. You will know when that is; a scar will have formed over the wound, you'll feel less vulnerable and raw, and you'll want to make the changes I'm suggesting in this book. So please, if you're living through the pain, take care of yourself. See your doctor, take care of yourself and your heart, and then return to me when it feels like the earthquake has stopped shaking your world.

LET ME INTRODUCE MYSELF

Hello, I'm Niamh, which is an Irish name, meaning 'bright/radiant' and pronounced in English phonetically as Neeve, which is due to the fact that we don't have a letter V in the Irish alphabet! From the outside, despite everything, it looked like I was doing alright. *"Resilient, strong, determined"* were all words I heard used to describe me and, for the most part, this made me feel proud. It's what I wanted to believe was true. I was chuffed that I had convinced those around me that this is who I was.

Only, none of that was true.

I may have been *all* of those things, but I didn't *feel* any of those things. I'd learned from an early age what was required if you wanted to fit in, to belong, to be accepted. I knew all the tricks and had not only practiced them, but I had become them. I don't ever remember asking or even considering what it was that I wanted to do, be or feel. I only remember measuring the reactions of others and delivering on the basis of those. I remember that piece so very well.

I was careful enough not to become a 'yes' woman. That would have been much too obvious. I presented a healthy mix of my own slightly less controversial opinions, and quietly became an indispensable right-hand woman. I'm guessing you could say I lost myself but, the truth is, I don't remember a time when I had discovered myself.

If I ever felt myself needing something different than everyone else, I'd tell myself that it was me who was wrong to want it. Amongst my family, with my friends and in my relationships, I was who they wanted me to be. I was so grateful for their presence in my life and did everything necessary to stop them from leaving me. I don't think that any of this makes me different to most of you navigating life. We do what we feel we have to.

From the outside, I was doing what so many young women were doing. I was gregarious, lively, fun and outgoing. I was growing into a career that I loved, in the city that I adored with a wonderful man by my side. I was an ambitious achiever with a wide network of friends. But the reality was that, by the time I had reached my late thirties I had, in fact, lost all of those closest to me. In the end, it simply hadn't mattered whether I was who they wanted me to be or not. None of that had kept them alive or in my life. That's where this book begins, because it's when everything began for me.

Hello there, I'm Niamh. I'm *the woman who lost everyone*. How are you today?

PART ONE

CHAPTER 1

MY STORY

Where you start is not always where you end up. I've seen this written several times, but recently I've started to question it. I'm not sure anymore that I believe it's true.

It's been my direct experience, that where we start is *exactly* where we end up. I started as a young six-year-old girl who loved her own company, felt so accepted and at peace, when it was her, her blank page and her pen. This young girl loved to write her thoughts to her imaginary audience. She also wrote words that she hoped one day might help others, but she also knew that not many people would ask a six-year-old for help. That girl has grown up to find true contentment in her life doing just that.

As I sit here, writing just after sunrise on this summer's morning, I'm reminded that what I'm doing with my life now and what gives me such joy is exactly what that younger me wanted, only she didn't know how to ask for it. The beginning starts where the finish ended.

I do believe this is where I was always supposed to be. That I just needed a few gentle, and some not so gentle, nudges along the way. If we each look back at how we started off in life, we will notice that the things we loved to do have a strange way of reappearing in our lives later, if we are open to seeing the signs and joining the dots.

So, who was I?

I was the woman who lost everyone she'd ever loved. I don't say this to be melodramatic; it's simply a fact. It's what happened. I lost everyone close to me, namely my remaining small family unit that up to then had consisted of my fiancé, my Dad and my Mum. They all died separately but suddenly in a short period of time, and I was thrown into a world of pain. I felt abandoned and I had no clue what to do next.

This is my story.

LOSING TONY

The year was 2005. I was engaged to be married to Tony. We had been together for almost ten years, so we couldn't be accused of rushing things. The wedding was planned for May 26th, 2006, the venue in Spain booked; and the *Save the Date* invitations had all been printed, written and posted out to invitees.

The day after they landed on people's door mats, some pretty big news landed on ours.

Tony came home from a week away golfing, during which he had played six out of the seven days. He was feeling great. Two days later, he was doubled up in pain and ended up in hospital so they could take his kidney stones out. It felt like a fair swap.

He was home two days later on Friday (*the days are relevant here*), only instead of getting better, he got worse. We were back to the hospital on the Monday, lots more tests done on Tuesday, and then on Wednesday the consultant came to see us and suggested we all go to his office. A nurse came too. The signs were there. Something was up. In those next fourteen minutes, everything changed for us. Our lives as we had known them were over.

'They found a tumour,' they said.

'It's in the pancreas,' they said.

'It's not looking good.'

They said nothing.

Nobody spoke.

I felt that my face was wet. I didn't realise I was crying. Tony sat beside me all strong and brave, squeezing my hand with such force.

He spoke next. 'What treatment can we begin with?'

More silence.

'Let's wait a while for that.'

Another sign.

You never wait with pancreatic cancer.

They knew. We knew.

That was at 17:53 hrs. on the evening of Wednesday 26th October. He died in my arms just nine days later at 04:04hrs in the early morning of Friday, November 4th, 2005.

I remembered hearing someone say that when someone is dying it's important to give them permission to go. These words could never have been truer than they were for Tony. He'd been very worried about so many things in his last few days as skeletons came crashing out of every closet. Me giving him the permission to go, telling him I would be okay, really mattered.

Tony had an awful lot of unfinished business in his life, a lot of unresolved issues, which are not my stories to tell here. He was worried, sad and terrified. Witnessing the person you love struggle with what they know is coming has to be the hardest part. I was helpless and could only watch as he lost control of all parts of his life. Everything became so intense and so painful, and it felt as if it was all just moving in slow motion. We never really discussed the fact that he was dying; he chose not to, and I respected that. The doctors had advised me to take his lead on this.

He'd slipped in and out of consciousness only a few days after his diagnosis. The ending came so quickly. As I held him on that last morning, reassuring him, I'm not sure I believed the words I was saying, but I was pretty sure that he needed to hear them.

I wanted to convince him that I was going to be okay dealing with everything, known and unknown, on my own after he was gone. I got up on the narrow bed, lay beside him, cradled him and repeated 'It's okay, it's okay, I'll be okay. Just let go now. There's nothing for you to be worried about here. I love you and it's okay.'

I know this reads like a cringe-worthy script from a Hallmark movie, but I swear to you that this is every word of what I said to him. I've no idea where those particular words came from, but they felt right for then. They were absolutely right for then. I had no idea that in that moment I was gifting him with the last earthly thing he would need from me and that was forgiveness, for the mistakes he had made but hadn't had the time to rectify, and for the unmet promises. I'm so deeply grateful I had the inspiration to do that, wherever it came from. The light came into that hospital room and into his soul at a time when he really needed it most.

This is how we love each other.

Being present when someone dies, I can only imagine, is like being present when someone is born. The only birth I've attended was my own and my memories of that, in fairness, are a little hazy. Death feels like such a uniquely tragic but lovingly precious moment, as you observe the change in their breath, the shallow intakes, the rattle, the silence between each breath when you wonder for that split second if they are gone, and then they breathe again and then the silence returns, but this time it doesn't get broken.

A baby's arrival is signalled by the welcome sound of a cry. A death is announced by empty silence.

I was aware that Tony had left his body. I was also very aware that he was no longer in pain. He was no longer suffering. He was no longer worried. I lay beside him talking to him, sharing what I knew would be our last private moments together. Getting up to leave that room and him in it was the toughest part.

Nothing about Tony's death was easy, but it is my belief that the web he had weaved accelerated his departure; but nothing would ever take away the deep love so many people felt for him. He was known for his wonderful warmth and humour and so it was incredibly fitting that we celebrated his funeral mass in our local Presbyterian Church, only to discover that afternoon that he was, in fact, Catholic! That's my boy!

That was 17 years ago now, but as I typed those words my face was wet again. That loss never leaves you. Rest in peace, darling Tony. Thank you for loving me. You will never, ever be forgotten.

Nobody I knew had died before, apart from my grandparents. I hadn't known what it was like to lose someone so close and whose future was so linked with mine. Not to mention feeling ill-equipped to be the one having conversations with medical teams about palliative care options. I was extremely out of my depth, yet navigating that time of my life was nothing short of a blur.

Of course, I see now that I was in shock at the speed at which it was all unfolding. It had come from nowhere and was clearly headed in only one direction. It absolutely felt like someone had taken over the controls on my life and I'd been relegated to that of a shocked passenger. A position I remained in for a very, very long time. The feeling of powerlessness overtook all else and I simply allowed myself to be pulled from one day to the next.

The months following his death were very dark and simply awful. Diving into that first Christmas just one month later felt like such cruel timing, as the world appeared to move on without any consideration for my pain.

LOSING DAD

I had an incredible bond with my dad. As a Veterinary Surgeon and a farmer, he had an intense appreciation of and love for animals and nature. Long before crèches were a thing, I was bundled into the back of his red Ford Cortina and we'd drive around the countryside, calling to farms every day. He had a penchant for very long rebel songs and so, pre-dating seatbelts, with me bobbing around in the back of the car, he'd teach me every line and verse of his favourite songs. To this day, I can still sing every line of 'The Town I Loved So Well'.

I could only have been three or four years old at the time, but I have some vivid memories of me peering up at the back of his head while he sang, with the green fields whizzing by. I can still remember the sweet smell of the countryside in the car – a result of the rolled down windows – and the dampness on my arms as I waved them about in the hazy rain.

When Tony died, Dad unsurprisingly kicked into total hero mode and, because he and my Mum lived 100km away, he took to phoning me every evening for a daily check-in. Anyone who knows Irish dads will know how unusual this is, built on years of having always had the phone commandeered by the woman of the house. But Dad was really hurting for me and I could feel that. My pain, I knew, was his also.

Two short months later, he announced he was coming to Dublin for a routine medical procedure and that it would be a good chance to see each other. I casually went to visit him that evening in the hospital, and for only the second time in my life, he cried in front of me. Things were not as 'routine' as he had led me to believe, or indeed as he himself had been told.

The consultant was worried about him. Very worried. He had a hole in his lung and it was getting bigger. Dad asked me to drive down home the following morning to break the news face-to-face to Mum. I wasn't sure what it was that I was supposed to say to her, but on the drive there I got the official call from the consultant where all my worst fears were confirmed. I was going to have to tell her that he was dying, and he had just months left to live.

That was Wednesday, March 1st, 2006. Dad died, with me beside him, once again, on Sunday April 9th, 2006, at 11:11am *(hand on heart, that's the true time he died!)*. That now too familiar change of breathing, the rattling, the long in-between silences and then the familiar empty silence.

Only this time when Dad died, something I find hard to articulate happened in that room that morning. Something I've not written about before. I did witness him leaving his body. Physically, to the eye, he had gone.

He had left his body, but I just knew he hadn't left me.

I'm still not sure if it felt so different because I'd always believed that Dad and I were connected, beyond being father and daughter. I'd always felt a deep soul-connection to him, but now I didn't question it. Nor was I sure if it was because I had no regrets. I had cared for him with my mother around the clock when he was sick; I had helped him carry out some important last wishes before he'd died, and I also knew that I had done everything possible to make him feel utterly loved by me. I knew he knew that.

Equally, I'm not sure if it was because I felt so thankful that he had lived for 75 years and had left such a wonderful legacy behind. I've experienced three close deaths, but his is the only one where I felt that. I know that for some this might sound strange, but with the benefit of knowing what I now know, I believe strongly that while his physical body gave up that morning it was his soul I could still feel present. It's his soul I still feel around me even to this day. He didn't leave that hospital room because his soul didn't leave that day. His soul lives on in me. I'm not sure of many things, but I'm sure of that.

LOSING MUM

When Mum died just a few short years later, it happened

differently but, in a manner, totally befitting her. She'd come to the hospital in Dublin on a Friday in early May, to experience two heart attacks quite unexpectedly a few days later on my birthday.

Almost two weeks later, the day before she died, she looked up at me from her bed and asked, *'I'm not getting ready to pop my clogs, am I?'* She looked relieved when I laughed and said, 'Oh for God's sake, the drama of it all.'

I'd sat peacefully by her bedside for those two weeks, rarely leaving. There was no drama. Which for us was rare, refreshing and beautiful, even if I knew that I was walking down this all too familiar path again. After one particularly gruesome day, where she was in a lot of pain and hallucinating from her medication, a nurse found me outside her door sobbing. I never felt more intensely alone before, or since, than I did that day.

The nurse asked me to take a little break and go home, have a shower, a short nap even and come back a few hours later. So, I did. Ninety minutes later I got the call telling me that her breathing had changed and to come back quickly. This time, as I drove back towards the hospital, something in me knew that I would be too late. I knew deep down that she wouldn't wait. Her fierce independence meant she would prefer to go on her own. Which is exactly what she did. She was warm when I got to her bedside, but she was gone.

The days leading up to her death, we had said our goodbyes in the only way we knew how. Awkwardly. She'd spent her whole life pretending to everyone that she was okay when she wasn't. But it was important for her to be able to leave as she had lived; in charge and calling the shots. She knew I was there for her right to the end. She knew she was loved.

LOSING MYSELF

You might think that because I'd been there before this time might have been a little easier. It wasn't. A lot of strange thoughts go through your mind when you lose so many people close to you, but probably the most unusual was this one: *'They're all gone, so thankfully now I have nobody left to lose.'* There was nobody now who I had to worry about getting sick and dying. Apart from myself, clearly, there was no-one left that had the potential to break me.

Following Mum's death, things started to feel really, really hard. I had no energy for anything, mental or physical. I was beaten and had run out of steam.

By the time Mum died, I was totally confused as to exactly who it was I was grieving over, and the guilt of that feeling was intense. I was really starting to resent that I'd only been given four months to grieve for Tony when I'd been pushed into caring for Dad and then subsequently grieving for him. After that, I'd been forced to change again and move into a much more supportive and hands-on role for my mum. The pain of grief really felt very physical, like a big lump of tar stuck in my chest. With her gone I didn't know what to do. There had always been someone else I needed to think about and to care for. There was nobody now.

Yet in all of this, who was caring for me?

This felt like a totally genuine question. The answer was nobody. Not even myself. Mostly, because I didn't let anyone ever see that I needed help and I certainly hadn't the first clue how to ask for it.

THE MIDDLE BIT

I call this the 'middle bit', because it's the tricky part between experiencing the losses and that time when you feel ready to start to heal. The time period is important here, in the context of this book, but also crucial in terms of how you respond to life. I didn't feel like I was ready to even consider healing until at least five years after Tony died. That's quite a long time when you think about it, but I don't want anyone to think that anything I'm talking about here should happen, or needs to happen, in the immediate aftermath of your life-changing experience. It takes as much time as you need it to take.

No matter what it is you are recovering from, you'll need time to process, integrate, grieve, recover from the shock, mourn your loss, acknowledge your pain, let it envelope you, allow yourself to be taken care of and all of that can take time. Everyone's timeline is different. There is absolutely no right or wrong in any of this.

Not everyone wants to hear that. Some people are genuinely desperate to hear that if you follow 'this' process and do 'these' things you too will bounce back quickly. Yet only you will know when you've stepped over that line, from wanting everything to be better to being ready to make everything feel better. Please take the time to consider where you are with this. Are you ready to begin rebuilding your life or do you perhaps need more time?

If you feel pressurised, or are putting pressure on yourself to come back to living this new life before you're ready, you're much more likely to slip back. It's called the healing process for a reason; you need to gently move through each stage at a pace that feels comfortable for you. You may need to revisit several stages over and over, but the most important thing is that you do what feels right for you.

Remember that this relates to all life-changing events and not just grief. Please don't think that if you haven't experienced something as extreme as grief you don't have a right to feel low, let down or in pain. I want right now to legitimise your suffering, your hurt, your disappointment and your loss.

If someone breaks your heart and you feel pressure from everyone around you to get back out there, don't. They want it for you because they want your pain to stop, and maybe (let's be a little tongue in cheek here) they may also want your moaning to stop, but listen to what feels right for you and more importantly *when* feels right for you.

All too often when we want to become unstuck, or feel like we need to start over, we find ourselves going directly to where we believe the solution lies at the point of change. The reality is that we would benefit so much more if we could learn to look at the environment we find ourselves in, so that we can understand what's blocking us and what is getting in our way.

Losing a job unexpectedly might, for example, change everything for you as it could force you to change directions. It can throw your plans up in the air and leave you with a crisis of confidence. You'll want to jump into action and start doing everything to find a new job by sending out multiple applications so that you can quickly fill the void. Yet, what if you're chasing a career that's not right for you, what if your skillset would be better matched to something else? What if your choice of career is making you unhappy because it was never actually your choice to begin with?

If you experience some health challenges and decide to

take better care of yourself, signing up for an intensive gym programme may not always be the best next step. You might benefit first of all from looking at the relationship you have with yourself – examining how you value your health, whether you make healthy food choices and understanding what is getting in your way.

All loss, all pain and all disappointments are valid. Whether you admit it or not, your problems are biggest only to you. That's not being selfish, that's being real. I encourage you before you rush to where you think the solution lies to look at the environment you are operating from, so that you can get greater clarity on exactly what you want, what is blocking you from having it and just what you need to do to get you there.

When you experience resistance, and you may in the next part of the book, it would be a little too easy for you to think, 'that's all very well for her, but has she lived through what I have?' You might genuinely be pleased that I feel better about my life now, but still believe that you could never see yourself moving on like I did.

You might even be extremely attached to the story that you are not one of those people who embraces change easily and, while you might love the idea of ending up in a better place than you're in, the effort it requires feels like too much for you right now. I get it, truly I do. We use lines like these to avoid having to deal with what's in front of us.

We like to convince ourselves that we aren't being told the full truth, that people are trying to trick us into believing we can come through this, when we know full well that we can't. But we can. You can.

Why so many of us find it hard to become unstuck and start over is simply because we are reminded of the past disappointments, losses, hurt, betrayal and failure to complete. This is what we are most afraid of experiencing again and that fear forces us to retreat back and avoid doing anything, rather than courageously choosing to do something. Sound at all familiar?

MY WAY TO THE MIDDLE

My way of coping through that post-chaos period was by filling my time, busying myself with everything and nothing. I moved between lying prostrate on my couch feeling sorry for myself and not wanting to see anyone, to going out searching for the answers in all the wrong places with many of the wrong people! The waves of emotion took me to extreme places and there was little comfort wherever I ended up.

I had become really lost and I'd no clue how to find my way back. I was pushing the self-destruct button and I simply didn't care. I had nothing or nobody left to lose and I knew it. That was indeed my crumbling. I had given up on myself.

I was the woman who bad things happened to, but now I was letting them happen.

MOVING IN THE RIGHT DIRECTION

Deeply unhappy, I had become utterly disconnected from myself. I didn't want to end up being the bitter, angry, jealous, resentful, wine-drinking party girl and yet it was starting to look that way. I had to make changes. Crucially, I was starting to really want to.

When you eventually reach that place, you discover that you have a choice. You stay there or you move away from it. The one thing I was certain of was that I didn't want to stay there. I was missing my curiosity and my sense of wonder terribly. I committed to change before I knew what the change would look like, because no matter what it had to be better, it had to feel better than this.

I was hungry to learn how I could do this. I bought books. I watched video trainings. I completed a course in Counselling & Psychotherapy. I studied and received a Master's in Reiki. I took a sabbatical from my Fundraising & Communications career and moved to Spain for a year. I'd love to tell you that I found myself there in Spain and that everything quickly and easily fell into place for me. I didn't and it didn't. But what it did mark was the beginning of the healing process and facing myself in the direction I needed to face to find my way out.

That year in Spain, five years after I lost Tony, also clearly confirmed that the career in Communications and Fundraising I had once loved and had invested over twenty-five years of my life in no longer fit my soul. I honestly had no idea why. It happened quickly, but I was in no doubt that it was true. We had simply fallen out of love with one another. I wasn't at all sure what I was going to do next; I just knew that this wasn't it.

I followed the breadcrumbs and acquired an Advanced Diploma in Executive, Leadership & Personal Coaching. I made what felt like a huge decision and formally resigned my position. That particular chapter was over. I didn't know what lay ahead but most notably here, I didn't need to. Knowing what I didn't want to do was enough. It was going to have to be.

MY ADDICTION

Sympathy can be addictive. I know this to be true. As a woman lost in grief, whenever I stood face-to-face with someone kind, I would see the sympathy in their eyes and hear it in their voice. I got so very used to it. I became so comfortable playing the role of 'poor Niamh' because it felt so safe and familiar. I knew the right words to put together, the correct expressions to make and how to be. It was true, I was now 'poor Niamh', and it led me to becoming far too attached to that moniker and finding myself stuck there five years later. I totally lost myself in this new identity and found it easier to exist there because it required little effort and demanded nothing of me.

I think I started to become more aware of how badly I was coping when the novelty of being the bereaved one, the girl who lost everyone, started passing. Those around me were moving on. I could feel it. I also could fully understand it. They had their own lives to live.

I was incredibly torn between a feeling of disliking the fact that people now looked at me with pity and being scared that others were starting to look at me with admiration that I had come through this. I didn't want to be pitied, but I didn't want to be admired either. I most certainly did not want anyone to think I had come through it. This time can only be described as extremely confusing, but I found myself, every time, embracing the role of the victim. I just couldn't help myself.

I began to question whether I was in danger of becoming addicted to the sympathy, only to discover that I already was.

I needed help. I needed to break out of this habit of always defaulting to victim mode. I see now that this marked the beginning of me moving to a more proactive and ultimately happier place, but I wanted to demonstrate here for you that my addiction to drama and sympathy had huge potential to really hold me back permanently.

It still does.

The difference is that now I am aware of it, I track it and monitor it on a regular basis and won't let it take hold again. I can't. A vast distinction exists between being addicted to the sympathy and the recognition that you are now ready to seek and receive professional assistance to take you forward. The line between both these states can indeed be quite blurry, and yet one is reactive – your addiction to sympathy; and the other highly proactive – seeking professional help.

You need to go through the reactive phase for as long as you deem it is necessary and right for you; but you also need to be open to considering the timing of being proactive when that feels right for you too. I like to call this the 'sick of my own voice' phase, where you can hear your inner voice say 'blah, blah, blah' when you start to tell your sympathy-seeking story.

I'll share more throughout this book how and when my addiction to sympathy and drama showed up in my life, but by naming it here I want to acknowledge that this is inside of you too, holding you back. Often without you being aware of it. Don't be surprised or ashamed of it, if you see it in you.

Please do remember to lean on those close to you who want to help you. They see you hurting and they may not always know what to do or how to comfort you, but don't shut them out. Just recognise that when the time comes and you know you need to step beyond this, when you can acknowledge that it has served you but that you are ready now to move yourself to a place other than this one, it's time to move. You are now primed to begin detaching from the drama.

WHO AM I WITHOUT SYMPATHY?

I didn't know who I was without grief or without sympathy. I hid behind the grief. We'll explore how you can so easily become disconnected from yourself in Chapter 3, but for now let me say that, before I was ready to see what had happened to me, I had to be able to accept that I had let it. This was the hardest part. This required me admitting to myself that I had become so dependent on the sympathy that I had fallen down a big hole full of self-pity. I had unwittingly become so attached to the drama, to the pain and misfortune of it all.

This was very new territory for me. I had spent my entire life working hard at appearing strong, looking like I had it all sorted and focusing more on the needs of others, which was in fact me doing everything I knew how just to be accepted and to fit in. Let me tell you, I was good. I played a blinder. I had convinced everyone that this was who I was because I thought it was who they wanted me to be. Hell, I even convinced myself, which was probably the most impressive part of all!

But here I was now really struggling and I had no idea who to be. Every day, I carried around the weight of those losses, the feeling of responsibility, the regrets, the heartache, the loneliness, the hurt and the pain. But I had refused to see that as the years moved on I was choosing to wear them everywhere. They became my armour. Nobody could get to me through them. They were me and I was them. Only I wasn't. I was so much more, and once I began doing what I could to put them down, everything started to feel lighter. I felt lighter.

It was time for me to stand on my own two feet again, to stop acting like the victim and give myself permission to live again.

I needed to remind myself of who I was when I wasn't grieving and be her.

WHAT HELPED ME GET STARTED

It feels important that I share here with you that it was also at this point in my life that I rediscovered something that had featured heavily in my younger years, which was my faith and my belief in something bigger than us all. This faith was not based on any specific religious belief but, long before I knew how to describe it, it was just a sense of knowing that I wasn't alone.

I felt then and do now that the universe indeed has my back. That there was and is something greater than us out there guiding us. For some, it can best be described as Spirit, Energy, Mother Mary, the Universe, Nature, Source, Mother Earth, Light, God or the Angels.

What you call it is irrelevant; it's how it makes you feel that matters. For me, that feeling of not being alone was what I needed to feel most when I was growing up and it was what I was starting to realise I needed again. I was right. It helped me a lot as I dived into the work of becoming unstuck and starting over. This work is much easier when you don't feel so alone.

THE FINAL BIT

Over time, I have learned how to become the very person that I myself needed when I was at the start of my own journey. Sharing my experiences, writing about how they have changed me, the tools I used together with the coaching and counselling qualifications I acquired, all now serve me to serve you. I know there are so many others like me out there who also feel lost, scared, angry, isolated and just need to be heard. You want to feel that someone understands all that you're feeling and how to navigate your way through it.

And I do.

Whether it's in my Group Coaching Programmes or in my RESET for Change 1:1 Coaching Programme, I have learned how to put the lowest points and the most challenging times to the best use. I spend my time now helping others just like you, to identify what it is in their life they want to change, and I inspire, inform and equip them with everything they need to go and do it. I consider myself extremely fortunate to be in a position to give this to them, but that same inspiration is what I also get from them too.

This is a story about how when you are ready you can, and must, reconnect and give yourself the permission you need to make changes in your life, so that you can move from pain to power with relative ease. This is for you when that time comes and you feel ready.

OVER TO YOU NOW

Right, so now you know my story, you have a strong sense as to why I feel qualified to speak about rebuilding your life and becoming unstuck. I hope you see that when I talk about moving from pain to power, it's because that's the exact route I had to take. It's also the same route I walk with each of my clients who have experienced setbacks in their own lives. It's hard, but trust me it's so much harder when you try to do it on your own.

I've shared my story; now it's time to focus on yours.

THOUGHTFUL TOOLS

Let me ask you this question and please answer it truthfully and from your heart – 'What is it that you are avoiding?'

You meet someone in a lift. You have until you reach the twentieth floor to tell them your story, describing who you are, what you are about and what you want in life. What would it be and how would you tell it? Can you think of one unexpected and positive outcome that has emerged from the setbacks you have experienced in your life to date?

CHAPTER 2

YOUR STORY

I've shared a big part of my story in the previous chapter, so now it's your turn. I hope that in opening myself up and revealing my story to you, you'll see what can happen when you allow yourself to become more vulnerable, when you let people see you as you really are, and that you are in fact demonstrating how capable us humans are of growing and expanding.

If you're someone like I was, who believed that to express your fears and insecurities was the ultimate expression of weakness, then I would ask that if you take nothing else away from this chapter, let it be this: it is only when you are prepared to let people see the real essence of who you are, of what makes you human, *including* your greatest worries and your deepest flaws, that you are allowing the world to witness just how strong you are.

You will soon discover that the more of you that you

reveal, the more of you will be understood, seen and heard. So much of your inner turmoil comes from *pretending* to be someone you are not, from responding to a false narrative that you must be someone else in order to be loved or more lovable. It comes from the constant pressure that you place on yourself to keep the facade up and that no matter what life throws at you you're able to cope, you are strong and resilient, even when you are neither.

For years, I clung to words like *'warrior' and 'survivor.'* I wore them as a badge of honour as I stumbled from drama to drama, and felt I must be performing well whenever I heard someone describing me with these words. As long as I was seen to be holding it together, the show would go on and everything would be fine.

Why did I do this? Because I believed that if they had a glimpse of how I was really feeling they would, like everyone before them, abandon me. In my terror of once again being abandoned, I totally abandoned myself. It took me so long to recognise this that it was only when I was willing to confess to not feeling so strong that I began the real journey back home to myself.

DO YOUR STORIES BELONG TO YOU?

You have a story to tell. I'm sure of it. What can be less obvious is where that story came from and accepting that you are being led through life by a story or stories that you've unconsciously subscribed to. Do you believe that right now, reading this, you're living out a story? Is it a story that represents a part of you or an aspect of you that you have been told, is you?

Someone may have told you as a child that it was safe for

you to ask for what you wanted, which led you towards being clear on your goals and desires throughout your life. Alternatively, you may have been taught that putting other people's needs first is an act of generosity and it's what good people do. If any of this rings true for you then maybe, just maybe, you could be one of those people who always do what you feel is expected of you. Do you also know that people who do this often go on to lead the life of a people pleaser?

You may have been conditioned by those in your environment to believe that you were either good or bad, generous or mean, kind or cruel, with no grey area in between. Yet, I believe it is deep in the duality of these beliefs that we can find the freedom to be who we are, while still always wanting to do good.

Whenever you emerge from a difficult time, ask only one question of yourself: *'did I do my best, given what I knew and how I felt?'* That's your measure, that's how you know you are learning and growing.

PAUSE & PONDER

- ✓ Can you see how the stories and patterns you believe to be true might today be influencing how you act and how you are perceived by others, and yet these may not even be *your* stories to begin with?
- ✓ How does that make you feel to think that these may not in fact be your stories, but that they were possibly passed on to you by someone else?
- ✓ Have you considered that you may actually have outgrown and outlived your stories? While they may have been true years ago, they no longer match who you are now, but you just hadn't thought to let them go.

Realising that the stories you are holding onto were never even yours to begin with can at first be quite confronting. It's possible also that you may not feel ready to accept that some of the stories you're clinging on to, in fact, belong to the person you were before your life-changing event, and that's okay too. I ask only that you become aware of it.

Maybe you're stuck where you are because you are trying to relive the story of who you were, before life gave you these challenges? You've told yourself that if you can just go back to being her, everything will be fine. But, and here's the difficult bit, that person doesn't exist anymore. She's gone and, in her place, there is a new you emerging.

That's what you and I are trying to do here; to help you see where in your life you are living out stories that are not necessary or even good for you. I want to clear the way for you, so that a rebirth of who you really are can happen. I invite you now to release the old stories, the ones that belong to others, the ones that aren't serving you anymore and, in their place, create space to start rewriting those for the person you are becoming.

IDENTIFYING YOUR STORIES

First, let's move you from that place of pain towards a position of strength and empowerment. Doing this will require you to acknowledge just what your stories are. This begins when you identify the stories that have always been there in your life, even if you are not aware of them, and especially if you are not present in them. You can get so consumed with the idea of what something 'should' look like, what others expect to see, and how something should appear that you totally disconnect from what it is in that moment and what it can be in the next.

In the aftermath of my own life-changing events, I believed it was expected of me to be sad, melancholic and reflective. Those rare times when I felt brighter or when I found myself considering something in my future, I kept to myself. Based on what I was convinced others expected of me, I was confused that I was even entertaining these feelings. How messed up was that?

Two years after my fiancée died, I met another man. I kept him very hidden. I didn't speak about him even to my closest friends, not because I didn't trust them but more because I didn't trust myself. The *story* I used to justify this was, firstly, that I didn't want anyone thinking I'd betrayed Tony's memory and secondly (and if I'm being honest, probably far more importantly) I didn't want anyone thinking I was preparing to move on. It didn't fit in with the narrative I had created or the one I believed was expected from me. Here I was, letting my life be dictated by an older version that was based on the alleged expectations of others. Incidentally, I did eventually go public with that 'man' and I even married him!

THE SOURCE

Next, let's look at just where these stories started. By identifying the source, you can then release the air from them and begin the creation of a new narrative. One that belongs to you and nobody else, and is in alignment with your values and your vision. One that mirrors the person you want to become. One that reconnects you with yourself as well as with your truth. This will only happen when you choose not to wallow, when you decide it's time to step up and fight back. When you declare that you are ready to rewrite and reclaim your personal power.

You taking back control is exactly what you are doing here. You are no longer allowing yourself to drown in a swirl of false stories; you are taking charge and creating a future that reflects much more accurately who you are now and who you want to become. This is you moving from a place of pity to true power.

CLIENT CONVERSATIONS – PENNY

My client Penny really struggled at the outset with knowing for sure which stories were hers and which had been foisted upon her by her parents, caregivers, ancestors, teachers, siblings, friends or colleagues. She had a good sense that none of these people had intentionally passed on their stories for her to carry for life, but she may have absorbed them and allowed them to become hers.

She'd enjoyed quite a privileged childhood. Her parents provided for her and her two sisters in every way possible. She never wanted for anything growing up and she believed that as a result of that she had a good appreciation of all that she had. This was true but it had come at an invisible price.

While trying always to teach her the value of money, Penny's mum had suggested that each time she received, someone had to sacrifice something just so that she could have it. You can see what her mum was doing here, and possibly see why she thought this was a good way to teach her daughter the value of money. But what it also did was create a 'money story' for Penny that for her to receive someone else must suffer.

On a deep level, this affected how Penny viewed money, her relationship to it, her ability to attract and keep it, and her feeling worthy of receiving it. It impacted her career, her financial planning, her ambitions, her relationships, how she rewarded herself and her sense of justice.

Regardless of its original innocent intentions, this story created a negative association regarding Penny's ability to welcome money into her life and caused intense money blocks.

Parents cause money blocks in their children not because of generational differences but also because of a belief that to respect something you must fear it. Without even being aware of it and with no mal intent, their money story can easily become yours. However, when you recognise this, you can then choose to address it and change your mindset around your right to be abundant.

During our time together, I worked with Penny on identifying her money stories, locating where they originated from (which was the easy bit) and then, through a deliberate series of exercises, changed how she thought about money. Working on the basis that 'awareness is healing', once we knew what had caused the issue, the rest of it took place without too much push-back. Penny needed to believe that she deserved to be financially wealthy if she so wanted. She needed to release the guilt she had always felt when she earned more money than she needed, when she got a bonus at work or received a generous gift.

She continues to be a generous person in all the ways that matter, but she is free from the story that for her to 'have' and to be abundant, someone else must suffer. They don't, and her rewriting that story helped her to not just see that but accept it as truth.

SO, LET'S NOW LOOK FOR THE STORIES IN YOUR LIFE?

When you first start to look for them, be aware that the most obvious ones will always spring to mind first, but I invite you to dig deeper and go beyond what rests on the top layer. What are the stories that you are carrying and living your life from right now? What might your version of Penny's 'money story' be?

Take out your journal and begin the process of identifying exactly what these stories might be for you. To make it easier, divide your life under headings such as family, love, health, career, friendships or self - whatever feels relevant for your life. This will help you separate the areas and give you more space to consider what stories exist for you under each heading.

JOURNALING PROMPTS TO HELP STIR YOUR INVESTIGATIONS:

- Do you believe it is safe to be you? If not, who, through their actions and words, showed you that it wasn't? And at what age(s) were you told this?
- Do you believe that doing what others want will make you more lovable?
- Did someone tell you to dim your light, not to speak up and certainly never to express your opinions or feelings out loud?
- Do you subscribe to the belief that to be successful you must work every hour and every day and push harder?
- Do you deserve to have money in your life?
- Were you told that to show vulnerability or to ask for help was a sign of weakness?

1. *Example of my Story of Friendship that I carried for years*

I believed that for my friends to want me in their lives, I needed to always agree with them and it was best if I kept my own thoughts and opinions to myself. This story originated when, as a child, I was told I was much too talkative; I had a tendency to talk far too much and this would make me very unpopular with others if I kept it up. So, I stopped. I learned how to balance appearing knowledgeable without disagreeing. I let others take centre stage and I sacrificed my needs for theirs. It felt easier. It was, for a while.

2. *Example of my Story around Career that I carried for years*

Success doesn't happen for people like me. It's for other people. If I keep my head down and do the work, I'll be okay. I'll never be the best but I'll always be okay. This story had its origins in my mother's belief that she was motivating me when she told me I had it in me to make a great number two in life. That I was smart enough, organised and engaging enough to be a great right-hand woman! You can see how this might have led me off course for a while. What I heard was that I didn't have what it took to be the best!

WHAT STORIES ARE YOU CURRENTLY LIVING YOUR LIFE FROM?

Of course, there are plenty of other examples, but these are the ones I've used the most with my clients, and in truth, these are the ones that have also featured most in my own life. I invite you to really watch out for recurring themes. You can learn so much from observing these and then reflect upon what fears you are carrying that could result in you not being honest with yourself or with those you care about.

Identify all your stories, small and big, significant and unimportant, irrelevant and explosive. This is about allowing yourself to go deep, to think about things in a way you most likely haven't done for years.

Once you locate each story, take a step back and look at them and then ask, are they true? Let the answer land. Don't rush it. Wait until you know you have listened to the most honest answer. Are they true now, today, or do they belong in the past? Were they ever your stories or were they passed on to you?

It's time for you to acknowledge there's a strong possibility that some of the stories you're living from are no longer true. In fact, they may never have been and you might be about to discover that also.

PAVING THE WAY

So far, we have identified and challenged some of the stories you have been carrying for years. What I want is for you to understand these and explore how you can begin paving the way for you to rewrite your own personal story, to build better boundaries, to reconnect with yourself and restore your confidence to find the courage within.

We've talked about the importance of creating space, but space to do what? Space to rewrite and create the life we truly want, rather than the one we are living now. When you don't know what you want to believe in, who you aspire to be, or what the next chapter should look like, you become susceptible to filling that void with a lot more drama, self-pity and sadness. This is why you desperately need to use this space to rewrite your story.

WATCH OUT FOR THOSE FALSE FEARS

In all of this, I want you to be careful not to ignore what scares you the most by pretending that it doesn't affect you. If you recognise that your fears, your doubts and limiting beliefs are all rooted in stories, that's a clear sign that they need to be investigated further. Your fears are very clever. They are as clever as your mind. They disguise themselves as elaborate stories providing you with false evidence as to why you should *not* do what you want to.

PAUSE & PONDER

Do you feel scared to match the expression of your words and actions with how you are really feeling inside? Do you attach endings to stories that aren't true, but which in your mind quickly become facts? *"If I do this, this will happen"*. *"If I say this, I will be judged"*. *"If I ask for this I will be mocked"*. *"If I say I deserve to be rich, I will look arrogant"*.

THE MIND LIKES NOVELTY, BUT THE HEART CRAVES FAMILIARITY

Any time you are in a growth phase, you are going to lose something. In this instance, you are losing what you cling to and that which keeps you feeling most safe. You're releasing the story that feels most familiar and that's hard for you. As you begin your rewrite, you'll start to realise that you are slowly emerging as someone new and that it's not such a bad thing after all!

How will you know this is happening for you? Well, perhaps the things you were once afraid of no longer scare you. Or, what if those things you so readily accepted and tolerated before no longer feel acceptable or tolerable? If, perchance, you notice that where once you remained quiet you now find yourself speaking your truth, or that feeling of needing to fit in is slowly being replaced with a desire to stand out, that's a sign you are emerging as someone new. Where once you were told to stay small, you now show up courageously; where once you may have been afraid to be visible, you now dazzle apologetically. Beautiful changes are happening.

When you have completed this work, your stories will then settle inside of you and offer lucidity. This leads you to make better choices and decisions, which will continue to stretch, change and transform you.

It is not that you have forgotten who you are, but that you have just not allowed yourself to remember who you want to be.

Rewriting your story requires courage. Courage to be vulnerable and be seen as who you really are. Courage to speak up, to stand out, to ask for what you want, to defend what you believe in, to practice bravely and to invite and welcome grace back into your life. Courage to recognise exactly what it is you are avoiding. You need to acknowledge as you do this that you are making great strides, and you should feel proud of the bravery you are displaying and the changes you are making.

CLIENT CONVERSATIONS - KATE

My client Kate was new to the concept of 'stories' when we started working together, so when I first put the question to her and asked, 'tell me what your story is?' she quickly replied something about being a wife, daughter and fundraising director who played tennis. She then smiled and raised her hands in a ta-dah kind of gesture, declaring 'that's my story!' Yet it wasn't. These were simply facts. They didn't reveal anything to me, which of course was her intention, albeit an unconscious one. That's the thing about our stories. We don't decide to misrepresent who we are with them, but we learn how to hide behind them to deflect attention from ourselves.

The longer the stories are in our lives, the less we question them. They become part of who we are and we don't challenge their veracity or even their relevance.

As a young girl, Kate's teachers described her as 'lively'. She loved to talk and she was quite the chatterbox, which was entertaining to her friends, but not to the teachers who were trying to manage a group of eight-year-olds. Kate had two siblings and was the youngest of the three. Her eldest brother had special needs and so much of her parent's attention, understandably, went on him. Kate also understood why this was necessary, but she'd also observed that it required her to dim her light a little bit more and to demand less attention than her parents had the time to give her. She believed the best contribution to the house she could make was to be 'less Kate'. And so, her story was written.

From that point on, in all areas of her life Kate presented herself as 'less Kate'. Any achievements or successes she hid well. She expected very little from her life and asked for little. She included apologies in most of her conversations and felt that her role was to support others, which she was happy to do.

As Kate entered her forties an unfamiliar feeling of resentment began creeping in. She started to question why so many of her friends and colleagues were moving forward in their lives while there she was, pretty much standing still. She wanted to feel able to ask for more, to simply want more, but had no idea where she would start.

It was here our work together began. My role was to guide Kate to recognise that the story she was living her life from wasn't serving her any longer, if indeed it ever had. I wanted her to see that she was living someone else's truth and that by silencing her voice at home, by choosing not to shine, she had extinguished the fire inside her that made her unique. I needed her to understand that nobody had asked her to take on the story of being 'less Kate', nobody had demanded it of her, she had chosen it and now it was time for her to choose a different version. If she would give herself the permission to.

Kate worked hard on doing this. She identified what had caused her to feel and think the way she did. She now knew when it started and how she had allowed it to continue. She saw that her intentions were pure, but she also readily accepted that they weren't serving her now and were in fact holding her back. The only thing blocking Kate was Kate herself and, honestly, I think she was mostly just relieved when she observed that.

We got her back on track quickly and, because it had all come from her, there was little resistance from anyone around her. What emerged was a much more self-assured Kate, unapologetic and unafraid to communicate her desires, to use her voice and speak her truth. And yet, the essence of Kate – her kindness, her sensitivity and her love of family – remained as strong as ever.

THOUGHTFUL TOOLS

Ask yourself 'what is it I want?'

And next, answer this... 'Is what I do, think, practice, how I behave, react and respond to things supportive of the life I say I want?'

What stories do you have imprinted in your mind of who you need to be to fit in, to be accepted and belong? Who would you be if you could let them go?

In your journal, write a few paragraphs on past experiences when you have not been truthful to who you are. Why do you think you denied yourself the opportunity to be much more 'you' and a lot less 'them'?

A REMEMBERING

"You feel safe when you are loved.
You love so that you can feel safe.
What if you believed that you are already safe to be loved?"

—Niamh Ennis

CHAPTER 3

DISCONNECTED

In the previous chapter, I went inward and invited you to identify the story (or stories) from which you are currently living your life. I helped you uncover which ones were true and which were false, which ones weren't serving you anymore and which ones were not even yours to begin with. I even got you to admit you were starting to display real courage!

You will likely already be feeling a shift. Can you feel it?

When you think about change, you act like there must be a specific problem and solution to it all. Yet often you don't need to know where the change is taking you. It's enough to trust that where you find yourself is where you are meant to be.

The difference between change and transformation is this: Change is changing what we do, transformation is changing who we are.

Change starts when you become more aware and when you have a better understanding of what's been blocking you, and what has been getting in your way. It is this that brings you on the journey from where you are now, where everything feels familiar and safe, to somewhere new and uncomfortable.

Now that you realise exactly what has been lurking behind your stories and patterns, you'll find yourself more able to name them. By naming them, you are paving the way to change how you think about them, how you feel about them and how you act on them.

CHANGE IS ALREADY HAPPENING FOR YOU

Let's remind ourselves of what you want to achieve as you move through this, so you can map out where you might need to stop off along the way.

- You want to detach from your drama and stop feeling like the victim.
- You want to feel empowered to do whatever you need to do to feel better.
- You want you to loosen your grip on trying to control every aspect of your life.
- You want you to create space for the light to return and surrender to this process.
- You want to believe that it is never too late to get unstuck.
- You want you to rewrite your own story and move from pain to power, with ease.

Right now, you're fed up looking at everyone around you *apparently* thriving, making bold decisions, grabbing new opportunities and accessing new possibilities while you are here feeling stuck. You feel life is passing you by and that there's nothing you can do about it. Of course, you know I'm going to say 'that's nonsense' and that there is definitely something you can do about it, but the word that I want you to focus on right now from this paragraph is 'apparently'.

This is another perfect example of a narrative you tell yourself – that 'other people are thriving and their lives are so much better and easier than mine'. But stop. Remember, it's only a story. One that you cling to and believe because it feels more familiar to you than doing something else, something new. The reality may well be, and most likely is, very different for them.

You don't ever know what is going on in other people's lives

You know what you see on social media is but a glimpse, an edited highlight of what they are willing to let you see. So too is the selective part you look at, when you tell yourself: 'You are doing less, you are not able to do what they're doing and this is why you are being left behind'. This allows you to slip back into the place of the victim and become more attached to feelings of helplessness and despair.

When you think about your own progress, it is all too easy to measure it against the pace of others and feel that you are coming up short. When you do this, you're simply validating your decision to stay where you are. You are justifying your decision to do nothing. In essence, you are ignoring the fact that your lessons, your experiences and your mistakes are unique to you. We all have different desires and goals. Just make sure that you don't get distracted or discouraged by those that belong to others.

HOW CAN YOU KNOW WHEN YOU ARE DISCONNECTED?

There are, in fact, lots of tell-tale signs that you have become separated from yourself. It shows up in so many ways but, let's be honest, few of them are ever positive. The ones we will explore here include people-pleasing, comparison, dimming your light to fit in, resentment, anger and even jealousy. If you've noticed an increased presence of negative thoughts and energy developing inside you, I'd wager that there's a good chance you might already be disconnected. That's the peculiar thing about it. You're rarely aware that it has happened. Until you are and it has.

To understand this more fully, let's dive into what it might look like for each of you.

YOUR HEAD AND YOUR HEART

The simplest way to describe how being 'disconnected' manifests is to first understand that we operate wholly as humans only when our bodies' two main centres – our heads and our hearts – are in total flow. Picture these two centres, or channels, with continuous energy flowing easily between them; that's what being connected looks like. When you are fully engaged, the two come alive and are wholly activated within you.

When you go to make a decision, you're looking for that place where you feel balanced between the rational and logical part of you (your head), and the emotional, feeling part (your heart). The very best decisions are a healthy mix between both, but a decision based on just one part alone is never good, and it's usually a sign that you're in a somewhat detached space.

To help appreciate them both a little more, let's look at them individually.

YOUR HEAD

It is here in your head that you do all your thinking, organising, planning and strategising. Think about all your checklists, what you need to do to stay on top of it all, consider everything that needs and demands your attention. This is where you manage all aspects of your life, your health, your finances and your career. When you study, read, access new information or learn something new, you automatically go to your head. It's from this exact space that you make decisions based on evidence, facts and what you absolutely believe to be true.

It is here all your thoughts and questions originate. This is when you find yourself wondering 'what do I do think of this?' or 'how do I think I should behave, respond or react?' You're unsure what you should do next or uncertain about how something should make you feel. You don't always stop to observe what you have learned from this experience or indeed what it is you believe to be true in this very moment.

You gather the evidence and you consider it to be the truth. You convince yourself that this certainty comes from your thinking head. Your head gives you total permission to defend your decisions. You make them coldly, dispassionately and based on what you believe to be hard facts, regardless of whether they are incorrect.

I know this to be true.
I can do this.
I have got what it takes.
I can do hard things.
I've got all the answers I need to do this myself.
I'm an independent powerful woman.
I've managed stress before.
If I stay here, I can protect myself better.

THE HEART

Where the mind is the operations department, the heart is inarguably the engine room, without whom there would simply be no other departments. It all begins and ends here. The list of what belongs in your heart space is not exhaustive. Nor is it the same for everyone. You should always allow for your own unique and individual tastes and desires. I've selected these because they are the most talked-about aspects, but just remember that they are not the only ones.

WHAT ELSE LIVES HERE IN YOUR HEART SPACE?

Love. Your ability to love and to allow yourself to be loved is here too. When you deepen your capacity to love, you are identifying what your purpose on Earth truly is; it is to love. To give and receive love. You become so much more capable of loving and receiving love when you open up your heart. Closing your heart may make you feel more protected and safer but it can also ensure that you feel quite isolated and separate.

You know that in the end 'nothing matters more than love' and you may understand that conceptually, but when this really lands and you *feel* it also, well, that's the power of love. Love creates but it can also destroy and lead to pain, loss, hurt and disappointment. The duality of love can both charm and scare you, but it should never, ever stop you from deepening your capacity to love, and be loved, by opening your heart back up.

Nature. As a child, I always felt very connected to nature. To daisies and trees in particular. It was something my dad had fostered and nurtured in me when he took me into the fields and involved me in all that was happening there. The May Altar was one such shared experience, where each year on May 1st he and I would gather up bunches of daisies, buttercups, bluebells and cowslips and place them on either side of the statue of Mother Mary in our home. This is a beautiful tradition that I still continue to this day with the exact same statue (albeit with half a litre of glue holding it in place).

Connecting with nature, however, does not simply mean getting fresh air into your lungs, although that is one of its known benefits. Nature is feeling free. What evokes and reinforces this feeling might simply be standing by an angry ocean, or in a windy whistling forest, watching an early morning sunrise or a clear starry sky during a full moon, placing our hands on an old stone, hugging a tree, planting our hands into some soil or digging our bare foot into the earth. This is when you remind yourself of the importance of nature and just how nurturing it is when you allow yourself to be immersed in it.

Intuition. Your instinct. It's a feeling. That feeling is best described as your inner knowing and is activated when your intuition communicates directly with you. The first challenge is being able to differentiate between the voice of your intuition and the voice replaying your past experiences. This requires you to be as silent as possible just in order to hear what it is saying to you. When you give yourself permission to really listen to this part of you, to the murmurs, clarity comes and your decisions are made with much more ease and trust.

It can also be difficult to recognise the difference between the voice of your instinct and what your desires are wishing to be true. Again, how can you know which is speaking to you? The idea that it's a feeling carries so much truth and yet it takes some real practice to be able to know what that feeling actually feels like. When you quieten the mind, when you slow down, you increase your chances of hearing its whispers. It may necessitate some perseverance on your part, but please do stick with it, as having access to your intuition is one of the most helpful and powerful tools available to you.

Creativity. Your love of birthing things into being. Acknowledging your ability to express yourself through music, art, words, crafts, writing, dance and gardening all begin here. Have you ever heard someone gushing about their hobby and your first thought was '*it's well for them that has the time!*'. More importantly, are you missing out on the chance to do more of what you love because you think you simply don't have the time? Why do you think it is that you prioritise all your chores and responsibilities, and then if you are lucky might find a spare bit of time every so often to squeeze in a hobby? Expression through creativity is such a joyful and powerful way to connect with yourself and the payback makes it incredibly rewarding.

Purpose. To truly identify with your most up-to-date reason for being here and to understand just what is going to give your life real meaning, it is essential that you fully align with your purpose. Purpose is a much-misunderstood word, but I would suggest that whatever it means to you is the correct meaning.

When you hit bumps on the road, there is a tendency to become fixated on discovering what your purpose might be, to search for that something that could help make sense of it all. Our purpose also has the potential to change as we evolve and grow. Living your purpose is most definitely the greatest gift that you can give yourself and, significantly, it will serve to inspire others to do the same, so you're right to go looking for it.

I invite you to really think about what the word 'purpose' means for you. That in itself can tell you a lot. Consider also what you suspect your purpose is calling you to do. In your journal, write down 4-5 points that you feel best encapsulate what you ideally would like your purpose to be. When I did this, I discovered that what I wanted my purpose to be was actually what it was. This involved among other things the prompt to share my own life experiences through the written word, which I simply wasn't brave enough to do beforehand.

What is it that lights you up inside when you think about doing it? Please don't overthink this. Let these questions land gently with you and observe your responses very carefully.

Spirituality. Because you already know that your soul lives here, it will come as no surprise to hear that your spirituality hangs out in this space too. That relationship you have developed with the Universe, Mother Mary, Spirit, Source, Gaia, Energy, Nature, God, whoever they are to you, it started here. When you feel connected to this, you will never feel alone again. Your understanding of this and how it impacts your life is very personal, so go inward for your answers; take the best of all you know and let your heart supply the rest. Connecting to that sense that there is something bigger, greater or wiser than you will, if you allow it, provide you with enormous comfort and support. So please let it.

You're there. I feel it. I feel you.
I want to be alone but never far from you
Remind me to thank you as often as I ask of you
I'm not quite sure who you are but I'm certain I don't need to.
You're there. I feel it. I feel you.

Prayer by Niamh Ennis

Vulnerability. For far too long we were told that showing our vulnerable side was a definite mark of weakness. Certainly, during my childhood we were taught to admire the strong, determined and capable women who did not let any other side be seen. They managed life's challenges with apparent ease and appeared like they could handle anything. If they got knocked down, they bounced straight back up. Phrases they studiously avoided using included: *'I'm not able for this'*, *'I've no idea what to do'* and *'It's beaten me'*. They clung to the idea of being warriors and stoics. Because that's just what you did.

While of course this accurately reflected a generation of fiercely strong women, which our ancestors were, it has to be acknowledged that it also allowed little space for being human. When you express your vulnerability, you open yourself up to receiving help and guidance. You are acknowledging that you simply can't do all of this on your own. You are calling out to your people and your community for assistance.

I personally have always found this one of the biggest hurdles to overcome. I believed that asking for help was drawing attention to my imperfections, deficiencies and limitations. The façade I'd meticulously created of being a warrior and a survivor would no longer make sense if I were to show that this other more human and flawed side existed too. How wrong I was! It was only when I found the courage to ask for help and was brave enough to share that I wasn't coping all that well that my healing journey truly began in earnest.

Hopefully, you can see now the essential work that is taking place constantly in both your head and your heart. But can you also see that, when you operate exclusively from your head and disconnect from your heart, you shut off access to these most important parts of you? What you are aiming for is to be able to continue to access both energy centres – your head and your heart. It is here you will find that elusive balance.

WHAT EXACTLY HAPPENS TO YOU WHEN YOU DISCONNECT?

When something challenging comes your way, your automatic instinct might just be to take charge of the situation. These life-changing events don't have to be something traumatic, but they will most likely be something you weren't expecting. You panic, you recoil, you shrink, you dim and you let your fire burn out. Quite literally, the wind has been removed from your sails and for a while you are in a state of shock.

It, *whatever it is*, has caught you by surprise. It wasn't expected and it most certainly is not welcome. As the shock wears off, you slip into coping mode. Doing what needs to be done to get you through hour by hour, day by day and week by week.

Survival for you becomes all about doing. It's how you know you're still functioning because you're getting things done. Simple things at first, like getting up, showering, eating, maybe even showing up for work or going out with friends. It's all about doing and distracting. You're taking control and in spite of all that is happening around you – you're still here. Months, sometimes even years later, you reflect on that time as one where you displayed courage and resilience. And you did. You survived it.

But what you may not have so readily identified is that in moving directly into the 'doing', you retreated back into your head. You closed yourself off from your heart. You avoided feeling. Your heart was broken, you were disappointed, let down, sad, worried and wounded. You did not and could not allow yourself to feel. You did what you needed to do to get yourself through those first few weeks and months. But the problem here, and I don't use the word 'problem' lightly, is that you totally switched off your heart and, in that moment, fully disengaged from yourself.

From that moment on, you were disconnected

The natural ease and flow between your head and your heart ceased. You closed off access to all those parts of you that reside in your heart; your feelings, emotions, ability to love and be loved, creativity, your purpose, your spirituality, your vulnerability and withdrew into your head space. It felt safer and you felt better able to protect yourself by feeling more in control. You were, at the same time, doing everything possible to avoid a recurrence of any future similar incidents.

Notwithstanding this, you were left feeling cold, isolated,

alone and lost. It's that sense that no matter what you do, or regardless of what anyone says to you, you can't snap yourself out of it. You're drained and you feel stuck. You lack any real direction and you simply haven't a clue as to what you should do next or what it even is you want to do.

You look around you and all you can see are others jumping forward with their lives, doing fun and exciting things. This triggers you. They trigger you. Witnessing their successes increases your capacity to constantly compare your life and achievements with people you've never or will never meet and forever coming up short. You feel left behind.

I'M NOT SURE I WAS EVER FULLY CONNECTED!

Oh yes, you were! Even as a small baby, you learned very quickly how to relate to your deep need to be fed, nurtured and loved. Can you remember that time in your life when you just believed you could have whatever you wanted by asking for it, and that everything in life was there to be enjoyed? Maybe, like me, you struggle with those very early memories, but believe me, all the science and experiential evidence points to everything being far simpler at that stage of your life.

To remind yourself just how you felt before life broke you away from you, why not try and conjure up those beautiful, familiar old feelings again? Revisit the places where you remember being at your happiest and most free. It could be the beach you went to on holidays, the green spaces you played in, the music you listened to from that time, the foods you ate that transport you back, or it could be the simple smell of a plant or cut grass that evokes the memory for you. Whatever that is, try and organise a visit to go there.

For me, the one place that instantly takes me back to that

feeling of safety, contentment and acceptance is amidst the trees. I feel the energy vibrate all around me when I'm standing there and I know just how blessed I am to live so close to the woods, allowing me to easily get my daily fix. Stepping in there each morning, I have been known to wander touching the trees and the stones, repeating the mantra *'I call all parts of me back home,'* which is exactly what those trees do for me.

By choosing to do what feels right for you, you are honouring your past self as well as your future one. This isn't about getting over anything; it's about stepping into who you are now, having lived through your own experiences.

THOUGHTFUL TOOLS

- Where in your life right now are you feeling most disconnected?
- What are your happiest memories of when you felt fully connected?
- What were you doing and who else was present?
- What do you miss most about that time in your life?

A REMEMBERING

I'm no longer focusing on what my brain thinks but on how my heart feels.

CHAPTER 4

STAY IN YOUR OWN LANE

This chapter and what I will cover in the following two chapters will give you clear examples of how the separation between your head and your heart manifests itself in your daily life, so you will recognise it when it is happening. If you find that none of these three examples resonate, which is of course possible, then I would invite you to reflect on a time in your life when they perhaps were present and to observe what you did at that time to navigate your way through. I've selected these three as they are the most prevalent, based on my clients' and my own. Now that you can better understand just what being disengaged means for you, how it happens and when, the next natural step is for you to acknowledge how it shows up in your daily life and what signs you should look out for that will inform you, convincingly, that your head and your heart have separated from one another.

When life throws challenging situations your way, you automatically kick into survival mode.

For some, this can be a positive experience, but others will find it a deeply disconcerting one. By exploring these very human reactions to life's bumps, my intention is to increase your awareness so you can learn how to navigate them in a way that makes you feel more empowered and better equipped to focus on your future.

COMPARISON

First up is our old friend comparison. There's very little about comparison I can say here that you haven't heard already. My intention is to show you how it always seems to present itself when you're feeling most detached from yourself. I want to show you how staying in your own lane and not looking at or being influenced by all that's happening around you can bring you home to yourself with more ease and flow.

There's no denying that, when you go to that place and compare the state of your own life against others, you rarely leave feeling better. This is not to say that you are always worse off than others, but it speaks to a false belief or perception that you don't have it as good as everyone else 'appears' to have it.

And let's be honest, we all do this to varying degrees, but let me ask you when the last time was that you felt a twinge of envy; or when you entertained the thought '*why can't I be that brave, lucky, wealthy, driven or loved?*' More recently than you might care to admit to, I'd guess!

I want also to demonstrate here, that not all situations of comparison are bad for you. If you're able to resist going down the rabbit hole and can instead turn these findings into an opportunity for growth and learning, the act of comparison can actually serve as an excellent motivator! So perhaps the next time you feel this, try and catch the thought before it fully blows up and ask yourself: '*what can I learn from this, what positive action can I leave with, now that I know this?*' Energetically, it will feel totally different.

I can't talk about comparison and ignore the very large elephant sitting comfortably with knees crossed in the corner of this room, which is social media and the Internet. You now have immediate access to the lives of others, and it is arguable whether this is a progressive step or a necessary evil. Before this, you relied on the verbal bushfire to keep you informed on how your ex was coping since the break-up; the holiday stories from your friend who stopped returning your calls months ago; or the big job your mum's friend's daughter landed, handing your mum a year's worth of ammunition. Now, you simply pick up your phone and, hey presto! It's there in your hand. The answer to the questions you didn't know you didn't want to know!

You are what you think.
But when you separate your head from your heart,
that is all you are.

When you're disconnected, the impact of comparison really intensifies. The reason being that your heart – your ability to love and be loved, your access to your own intuition and creativity, your potential to be vulnerable and ask for help – are all currently closed off. You shut them down.

Right now, you're living with only the activities of your mind to navigate your way out of this. You receive information about how others are thriving, changing, moving forward with their lives and you instantly think, '*Why isn't that me?*', '*Why am I so stuck?*', '*Why am I never able to do brave things?*', '*What's wrong with me?*'

You focus on what everyone else is doing and end up ignoring what it is you need to do to for you. You overthink everything because you're unable to distract yourself by doing what inspires you creatively. You bottle it all up inside of you. You won't dare share your concerns with a loved one and be vulnerable. You won't ask for help. Ever.

This leads you right back to that false belief that the success and achievements you witness others receiving will mean that there are less now available for you. This is not true, but you allow yourself slip into that negative way of thinking and, in your own mind, this provides you with the justification that you're safer doing what you do because it's protecting you! But is it?

Let me present a more realistic alternative. I say 'realistic' because I'm not going to try and suggest that when and as things improve, you won't experience some comparison. You will. The difference is, however, that when you are connected and in tune with your heart and your vulnerability, you are more able to grasp that other factors might also be at play here.

1. Have you ever compared someone else's relationship to yours?

Respectfully, that doesn't make sense. Only you know what happens in the privacy of your relationships and you may be overlooking that while your partner might not be perfect, they are perfect for you. Your heart will tell you that, so listen.

2. When your friend makes a big life announcement about

something new and exciting, is there a tiny little part of your heart that sinks and wonders when will it be your turn?

Honestly, that's really okay if there is. As long as you are able to celebrate her joy, it might mean that yours is on its way and when it arrives, you'll be totally ready for it. Your ability to trust will help you here.

3. *When was the last time you found yourself feeling frustrated watching someone in your space soar? You want to be the success that they appear to be, but it's not happening quick enough for you.*

It's natural that you might feel a little unsettled and insecure when it comes to your own life, career and business, but acknowledge that they were once where you are now and this will actually serve as an example of what lies ahead for you. To help, repeat this mantra: *'this is great to see, my time is getting closer!'* It works for me!

These examples are not to demonstrate how to avoid comparison, but more importantly how to live well with it. They will hopefully show you how staying in your own lane and being connected to yourself opens up more doors and creates greater opportunities for growth, in spite of your feelings of discomfort.

CLIENT CONVERSATIONS – AMANDA

When Amanda first came to see me, she was looking to change her job. She worked for a very large well-known multinational IT company. She was, in her own words, 'miserable in that toxic environment,' but she lacked the courage to take any action to change.

She didn't know where to begin, having made several false starts before where the fear always won out. Fear of never discovering just what she should do, fear she wouldn't get another job, fear she wouldn't be able to meet her bills, fear of what others would think and say. She'd been made redundant years before, and could not handle going through that experience again. So, in the absence of courage, she stayed.

During one of our sessions, I put this simple question to her: 'If you weren't so afraid of what others think, if you knew no matter what that you'd always be able to pay your bills, what is it you would like to do?'

We explored several possible options based on the information she had shared in previous sessions, mostly relating to her childhood, and to the things she loved doing. These provided us with a great starting point. One thing kept jumping out, no matter what we were discussing, which was how preoccupied she was with what each of her former colleagues had gone on to do. She referred to it constantly. I couldn't say that it presented itself as jealousy per se, but there were some very definite 'envy' tones in there. Without realising it, she was constantly comparing 'their progress with her stuckness' and it was this that had paralysed her from moving forward.

Her previous experience of having been made redundant had caused her to become disconnected from herself and so all her decisions were now being made from a place of fear. (The obvious exception here was her asking for help by working with me, but in fact it was her husband who had booked this for her!).

So, there was quite a lot going on here, but let me briefly summarise where we were before we decided where to go next.

Amanda had experienced her own challenging life-changing event. Her redundancy had been totally unexpected and left her naturally quite nervous about her financial future. Her confidence had been shattered. Her childhood money stories of never having enough had been reactivated. She was determined not to find herself in this situation again, not to be caught off-guard like this, and so she disconnected and went into full-on controlling mode. It served her well, for quite a while.

As she watched her colleagues leave to grow their careers, she found herself feeling envious and forever comparing her life to theirs. 'Why could I not be more courageous?' 'Why are they able to generate such great success in their lives and here I am stuck and so scared?' 'Why them and not me?'

When we started working together, and I explained the concept of just how we become disconnected from our hearts in order to protect ourselves, she told me afterwards in her own words: 'that's when the fog started to shift.' I'd never heard it described like this before, but now that I had, it made total sense. 'I was disconnected.'

It took us a while, but the first step was helping her to see what was behind how she was feeling, so she could fully understand it. Then she had the choice. She could choose to stay there, feeling as she was, or she could engage in some practical next steps to change all of that. Thankfully, she was curious and she chose to change. She chose courage over fear.

Through utilising many of the tools I'll be sharing with you in the second part of this book, along with being open to receiving some extra doses of ToughLove Energy, she did just that. She allowed herself to access her vulnerability and in doing this she opened herself up to receiving so many more options and possibilities.

Not least, she reunited with her heart and rewrote her story. All because when it came down to it, she refused to let her past determine her future. We spent some time working on finding what it was that lit her up and I won't pretend that it happened quickly for her (it didn't), but when it finally landed she was sure that she had found what she had been looking for all along.

I feel that I must let you know this last piece, as it happens more often than you might imagine, but Amanda stayed in the same company. She moved to the Design department so that she could focus full-time on one of her passions. (Her long-term plan is to create her own business but she is taking it one step at a time). I know this is popularly referred to as a career pivot, but I prefer to think of it as Career Correcting!

Amanda wasn't miserable because of where she was working. She felt like this because she was protecting herself and staying with what felt familiar. It felt like her only option and the safest one. I helped her see that it wasn't.

Her propensity to constantly compare her life with that of her colleagues and friends was the exact sign she needed to reveal that she had shut herself off from her heart space, and from there we could refocus her time and energy into designing a new future for her. In every meaning of the word! I got her to see beyond the fear and showed her what a difference it would make in her career if she allowed herself to reconnect with her creativity and vulnerability. That's where her particular powers lay. It was like putting on a pair of glasses. Suddenly she could see in front of herself so much more clearly.

STARTING OVER – BUSTING THE MYTHS

Many of us assume that when it comes to starting over or becoming unstuck, it must mean starting from scratch. This absolutely does not need to be the case. Starting over means taking the very best of your past experiences, your wisdom, and your learnings and bringing them with you enthusiastically into the next chapter of your life. Realising that can honestly feel liberating.

- What have you done in your life that makes you feel so fulfilled?
- If you were being honest, what about you is so beautifully unique?
- What are your strengths?
- What got you here?

Take a look back over your shoulder, acknowledge all that you have done, all you have survived, all you have coped with and be proud of it.

Instead of thinking about what others have that you don't have, try to remain focused on all that you do have. Stay in your own lane. Remind yourself that you do not have all the facts and you don't know what's going on for them behind the scenes. Because you don't.

To believe otherwise is to play the victim and you are most definitely not the victim here!

Face up to the fact that, yes, you can get lost in comparison and, yes, there will always be people who 'appear' to have more of what you want, but have you thought that you might be that person to someone else? We will never all be at the exact same level at the same time, it's simply not possible.

When you compare, you're immediately relinquishing your power and placing it into the hands of others. You are sending the message out to the universe, loud and clear, that you believe you are not worthy of good things; you don't deserve them and that you're unable to receive them.

Your life has too much potential for that to happen and that's the message we want the universe to hear from you. You are done with your sadness and you are ready for the madness! This part of the process is all about moving you from pain to power; to the place where you will have detached from your drama and are no longer a victim of it, and that's exactly why you need to do all you can to stay focused on what's happening in your life.

THOUGHTFUL TOOLS

- If you believed anything was possible for you, if you listened to your heart and heard exactly what it was saying it wanted more than anything, what would that be?

- How would you feel if you were to have it?

- How would you show up in the world?

- What three achievements in your life are you most proud of?

- How did you feel when you set out to secure them?

- How did you feel when you got there?

- What's getting in your way of believing that you deserve and are worthy of having all that you want?

- What steps can you take now that will help you to stay in your lane more?

CHAPTER 5

SHOW UP AND SHINE

'Light up no matter who is around you. When you do, you make it easier for your people to find you'
—Rebecca Campbell, Light is the New Black.

Have you ever watched others thrive and it made you shrink? You know that feeling when their success seems so far away from where you are in your life that internally, silently, you give up? You decide in that moment that you can't compete. You resolve to stay right where you are. It feels easier there. You won't have to deal with any future disappointments or setbacks. You abandon your dreams and your ambitions in that moment because you've decided that what you were considering were just fanciful notions.

If this scenario even sounds slightly familiar, then you most likely know what it's like to opt to play small and dim your light to fit in. But do you also know just what it is you risk missing out on, by doing this? The lost opportunities because you felt you weren't good enough or, to be more accurate, that someone else was better. The missed chances you let slip away to show up and shine because you were afraid of how it might look.

When we dim to fit in, we become less of who we are, and certainly, much less of who we want to be.

Whether it's that you're someone who is easily influenced by the opinions of others or were silenced by a dominant presence earlier in your life, the practice of dimming your light should never be mistaken as a proactive move. It is not. It is entirely reactive and not at all healthy.

When I was younger, an adult repeatedly told me that nobody liked being around a chatterbox. It was pointed out to me that I was prone to interrupting others, that in my excitement I frequently talked over people and took far too much airtime for myself. In no uncertain terms, I was told I was much too 'gobby' and simply needed to stop speaking so much. **I was just eight years old.**

While I accept that they were possibly trying to package this as helpful advice for my own good, what ended up happening was that my spirit was damaged. It taught me that what I had to say, *nobody wanted to hear*, and that I needed to be cautious when it came to speaking up. It was not safe for me to express myself openly and naturally. As a result, I learned to keep my real thoughts and opinions to myself, not because I wanted to but because I believed nobody wanted to listen to them. I stopped shining.

I feel deeply grateful now that I went on to find another

way to express myself, which was and still is in writing. With a pen in my hand, the thoughts in my head can go straight to paper. I don't have to think about them, edit them or question how they might turn out. I'm not worrying, 'will they offend anyone', 'upset anyone' or 'contradict anyone?' I'm certainly not asking, am I interrupting someone or saying too much?

I invite you to examine where in your life you might be dimming your light and then to ask, why that is so? There is something behind this, and you need to understand what that is and when it started for you.

- Has a life-changing event or disappointment you may have experienced in the past caused you to believe that it is safer to dim your light?
- Have you ever experienced criticism for being too much; too loud, too obvious or too confident?
- How do you express yourself with your family and friends? Think about where in your life you are feeling too scared to shine.
- Do you ever feel overlooked in your career and where are you a little hesitant to offer your personal opinions or suggestions in the workplace?

For many, the potential of criticism or judgement can simply stop you from being seen or heard. Be honest when you reflect upon whether your life is in fact full of you doing lots of insignificant stuff to avoid having to confront the real issues.

- Does criticism crush you and convince you to use your voice less?
- Does the threat of being judged or mocked paralyse

you?

- Who do you speak to when you need to share?
- Where feels safest to be you?

When you've ruminated over these answers, I encourage you to give serious thought to what you could do now to give yourself the space to be who you are?

So why do you dim and not shine?

I believe this mostly comes from a genuine place of fear. The fear of being abandoned. The belief that if you don't dim and choose to speak up, to shine, to express how you really feel or do what you really want, then you face being criticised, judged, rejected and left alone.

You dim because you believe that if you don't you will be punished and less lovable. Dimming makes you smaller, less noticeable. You also dim because somewhere along the way someone told you it was safer not to shine and that perhaps you didn't deserve to be fully seen or heard.

When you find yourself dimming your light, the chances are that you blame others for the fact that it's happening. Yet, and this may sound harsh, when you stop blaming other people and take responsibility for your own choices, you'll start to feel much stronger.

When you stop being who you think they want you to be, and start being whoever it is you need to be, that's when the freedom comes. That's when you find your light again and really learn how to show up and shine!

HOW TO KNOW WHERE YOU ARE DIMMING YOUR LIGHT

Is it happening in your career?

✓ Have you ever found yourself playing down what you can do for fear of outshining someone else (a colleague, a sibling or a friend)? Can you think of a time when a manager dismissed a thought you had, only to represent it later on as their own, and you said nothing despite feeling quite hurt? This happens more than you might think! Think of those times when you may have stopped yourself from speaking up or showing up as you wanted, purely because you were afraid of being judged.

✓ Have you witnessed a colleague receiving unnecessary and unwarranted criticism at work for simply expressing their views, and you said nothing? Looking back now, you realise that you should have spoken up and feel quite remorseful for your silence.

Is it happening with your family or friends?

✓ Can you recall a time you wanted something new and better in your life? You decided it was time to do something about it and make some changes, but were instantly made to feel guilty by those closest to you who felt unsettled about your desire to change? So, you retreated and did nothing. You told yourself you needed to focus on what you have now and not what you could have.

✓ Have you left a gathering of your friends feeling rather

flat and not at all good about yourself? Do you find yourself talking less about the things that really light you up, that interest you and spark excitement in you for fear of being laughed at or judged by these friends?

✓ Have you found yourself feeling less comfortable with how someone speaks to you in front of others, commenting on your appearance or making snide remarks, but you don't want to upset them and appear precious? So, you put up and shut up.

These are everyday examples that I hear about regularly in my practice. They are, yet again, more evidence of what happens when you are disconnected. When you dim to fit in, you are in fact placing your own sovereignty into someone else's hands. You may not identify fully with being a victim, but you equally feel powerless to stand your ground and so do everything that makes it impossible for you to show up and shine.

You allow others to speak to you and behave around you in an unacceptable way and do very little to change it. Why, because you are scared of what their reaction will be if you push back and reclaim your space. To get beyond that fear and stop disrespecting yourself, you must identify and fully understand the source. So, let's explore this a little further.

WHERE DO YOU COME IN YOUR FAMILY?

Have you considered that perhaps the order in which you were born – where you come in your family, how you were treated and how others within the family treated you – can determine your propensity to go on and feel called to dim to fit in?

At family gatherings, it is not unusual that you will revert back to your childhood role. Think of the annual Christmas dinner. As you sit with your family, observe how each of you slip right back into the roles you created as children. Within families it can also become accepted that you tolerate behaviours that you would never accept from someone outside, so you might want to watch out for that too.

My role was to be the chatty one. The entertainment. Yet, I can't honestly say that I always felt safe to speak freely. I had been told that being chatty wasn't necessarily a good thing and so as I became more self-aware. I found I spoke less and when I did, I censored what I was saying. In my desperation to fit in, I worked so hard to please that I performed, and during those performances I lost myself more and more.

This continued well into my adult years until I became aware of what I was doing and more importantly why I was doing it. Only then did I choose to stop. These days I say what I want and I also have got so much better at staying silent when that's what I feel like doing as well.

WHAT HAPPENED TO YOU AT SCHOOL & IN YOUR TEENAGE YEARS?

This is significant because it was probably the first place where you witnessed how the dynamics of relationships outside your family worked. You watched and were part of some friendships that functioned well (and more that didn't), and you quickly observed the importance, the absolute necessity, of being liked and accepted. It was here you learned how to fit in and how not to stand out.

From there you moved into your teenage years, which were so full of contradictions. This life phase had you wanting and needing to be the same as everyone else. You tried so hard to blend in, to be part of the same thing that everyone else was. These were your formative years, where you tested the benefits and drawbacks of being accepted. They were indeed some of your toughest days.

WHAT WAS THE WORLD TELLING YOU THAT YOU SHOULD DO?

To be fair it was pretty clear. There was an order to things. A list of 'shoulds' and 'should nots.'

You go to school, then if you're lucky enough you go on to college, get your first job, meet a few potential life partners, settle, buy a house, get a dog or have children, take care of your parents, keep in touch with your friends and every so often check in with yourself to see how you're doing. Bury your parents, bury your friends and bury your partner, until it's time for you to be buried.

And yet I'd argue that of the 100% of people who follow this route, 50% of them are on the wrong path, 30% of them realise it and 5% of them do something about it. If you're reading this, I'm going to guess you are in the 30% who realise it and are aiming for the 5%! You still with me?

TIME TO MOVE ON, PERHAPS?

If you find that others make you want to shrink, be less you, hide and step back then maybe, just maybe, they are not your people and you are not theirs.

Maybe, regardless of the history or the connection between you and them, it could be time to revisit how they make you feel and give yourself space to grow, to expand to be bigger, louder and more of yourself. When you step into who you are now, you're creating space and inviting more of your own people to find you. And they will find you.

By choosing to become more *you* and less *them*, those already in your world might start to feel a little uncomfortable; they may not respond well to you changing. *Remember, while they might not be ready for change, you are.*

It's critical that you surround yourself with people who genuinely want to see you thrive, expand and grow. They must want this for you. If your desire to change changes how they are with you, then please don't let it stop you. Gently move away and move forward. It's your time to shine.

PLAYING SMALL IN CLOSE RELATIONSHIPS

You might think that playing it small doesn't happen so often in close relationships. Sadly, you'd be mistaken. So much so, that I've received permission from my client Cathy to share her story here.

CLIENT CONVERSATIONS – CATHY

Cathy met Liam in their second year of college. They met when she was twenty and he was nineteen. They dated throughout college, took a year out and travelled to Australia. On their return to Ireland, Liam did his Master's in Engineering and Cathy took up her apprenticeship with a solicitor's firm. They worked and partied hard for the next six years, and then on a New Year's Eve night, Liam proposed and (in her own words) made Cathy the happiest woman alive.

She had three sisters, she was the youngest by five years, and that gap had always made her feel a little uneasy and left out. Her whole life, she had felt like she didn't quite belong in the family she was in; it was only a feeling and, considering they all shared the same fire-engine red hair, she knew there was nothing more to it than that. But this feeling caused her to be driven by a desire to blend in, to fit in and it stopped her from doing anything other than what was expected of her.

She'd craved a relationship like this one all her life. She'd had that sense of never quite feeling whole on her own and she'd shared this with Liam from the start. They married, had a miscarriage a year later and three years later had a beautiful baby boy, followed 18 months later by another. 'Irish twins', she said this every time! She knew from the outside she looked like one lucky girl, and she was. She loved her career and felt very fortunate to be in a position to keep doing it. Her mum and Liam's mum both lived close by and, with the help of an exceptional childminder, their life was busy but happy.

Cathy's fortieth birthday came and went, but she often recounts that it wasn't long after that when something inside her started changing. She's at pains to point out that nothing in her external world appeared to be any different. Liam, the kids, her mum and her pals were all great. It was her. Whatever this was, it had happened to her. Something inside her had changed. Liam suggested that maybe work had become too stressful, but she felt flat, disinterested, unmotivated and quite fed up. She first came to see me around that time. She'd read an article I'd written in a magazine, where I talked about that feeling when you know something is wrong, but you just don't have a clue what it is or what to do about it. That was when we got to work on 'Project Cathy'! Our first aim was to discover what was causing this feeling of 'meh' and 'bleh' and then, when we knew what it was, we could put a plan together to address it. Sounded simple enough! Only it wasn't.

Cathy felt so incredibly guilty every time she heard herself say something that made her sound ungrateful or unhappy. She was very aware that she had a privileged life and a good one. So why was she feeling like this? What was causing it? What was behind it and how could she get beyond it?

She admitted to me that she'd started dreading going into work. She found herself being irritated for the first time not just by her clients but also by her colleagues. Everything still pointed to her being dissatisfied by her job. But she knew there was more. Quite a bit more in fact.

Hidden grief

In conversation one day, Cathy passed quickly over that time when she miscarried. We talked about grief, shame and the challenge of not feeling able to talk about some events because they make other people feel uncomfortable. I asked her if she had been able to speak about her miscarriage, but before my sentence was finished, she was sobbing. I organised for Cathy to speak to a bereavement professional about this, which she did, and we paused our work together while this was happening.

This helped her process a lot of things that she had hidden and buried inside her. She had suffered a major loss in her life and had not felt able to give herself the space to grieve. This grief was blocking her, holding her back and at the same time, it was also doing everything it could to make her notice it was there.

I recognised these signs. I knew that when something keeps resurfacing and you don't deal with it, it simply reappears somewhere else in your life. It doesn't go away until you acknowledge it. Healing begins only when we face something; if you convince yourself that you need to get over it and move on, you are simply sidestepping. Cathy was sidestepping.

She had become totally disconnected from herself. She had disappeared into a box-ticking exercise in her life that, without realising it, everything she did came from her head space. Her organising, planning and coping skills had all been focused on looking after and taking care of everyone in her life – except herself. In trying to remember everyone else, she had forgotten herself.

Lacking purpose

When I first asked Cathy to share with me what she felt her purpose was, she was honest and said she didn't have a clue! What emerged over time was that Cathy had just followed the path her parents, her teachers, her sisters, her friends and her colleagues had travelled. She'd ticked off every box that was expected of her and had done it all by the book. 'But I have a great husband and adore my boys so what have I honestly got to complain about?'

The final outcome didn't result in Cathy turning her life inside out. It actually started gently. One of the parts of her career that she loved the most was when she'd get the opportunity to mentor a team member. So, she decided to enter into an external programme as a volunteer, to do just that for other women. The payback was immediate. She felt such a strong sense of purpose and instantly saw how being of service to others was a gift that she was also giving to herself.

She later went on to seek further qualifications in this area and is now working part-time as a solicitor and part-time as a mentor, with the long-term plan of being a full-time Business Mentor.

Liam, of course, rowed in behind her. Eventually. In fairness, it didn't take him long to see that this was something she really needed to do, for her. He suspected it was going to happen whether he liked it or not and he really sat with that new feeling of her making her decisions on her own. With Cathy's reassurance, it got much easier for him and he accepted that this was about her sense of purpose, her choices and her happiness. And in the end, that's what actually mattered to him too.

By asking herself exactly what it was that she wanted and listening to what she heard in response, she had honoured herself. No more dimming to fit in.

THOUGHTFUL TOOLS

- If you weren't so afraid of what others think, if their opinions did not matter, if you only did what it was that felt right for you, what is it you would do with your life?
- Where in your life do you not feel safe to speak up and be the full version of yourself?
- Who are you not being that you cannot keep hidden any longer?

A REMEMBERING

When anyone asks me now, 'give me one of your best qualities', I reply, 'I'll never fit in'.

You need space.

Space to let go so you can welcome in more

Space to say goodbye before you feel ready

Space to receive love when you feel fear

Space to detach from the drama and move on

You need it because you deserve it.

It's your time.

CHAPTER 6

PEOPLE-PLEASING

We teach others how to treat us by how we treat ourselves. If we are constantly people-pleasing and are always so quick to revert to our people-pleasing ways by putting other people's needs ahead of our own, then what is that saying to others about how they can or should treat us? How can we expect them to prioritise us if we aren't able to prioritise ourselves?

Recently, I saw a post online where someone wanted to know exactly what constitutes a people pleaser and the answer almost made me snort. It went like this: '*A people pleaser is typically someone everyone considers helpful and kind.*' I laughed because it felt like the most gaslighting answer you could possibly imagine. '*A people pleaser is someone everyone considers...*' And that's the truth about people-pleasing. It's not about what **you** might think or how **you** might behave; it is about how your actions are seen, viewed and judged by **others**.

Personally, I much prefer this less inflammatory description of what a **people pleaser** is and how you can recognise if this is something that you do:

> A people pleaser is someone who constantly does everything they can to make others happy. They'll often go far out of their way to please someone, even if it means making personal sacrifices and using up their own time and resources.

When you think about it, at its most basic it is you choosing to put someone else's happiness ahead of your own. You might have your own reasons for wanting to do it, but at its core, it's the very real desire to please someone else before you please yourself. It can be difficult to fathom if you're in that unusual cohort of people who've never experienced it but, for so many who can, the difficulty starts in earnest when you try to change your ways.

You might notice that certain people bring out the people pleaser in you more than others, which, as an observation, is a healthy one. I also strongly believe that there are people-pleasing traits and features that are in reality terribly endearing and speak to the inherent kindness that exists in us all, and these should be protected at all costs and never removed. We should always feel free to want to treat someone else well and to simply do good things for other people, with no other agenda.

However, the reason I talk so much about people-pleasing is that I believe it's at the core of what blocks you and stops you from moving towards becoming who it is you really want to be. When you are feeling insecure, frustrated or fearful it's easy to hide behind your people-pleasing ways and, yet, until you confront them you won't be able to make much progress. When you doubt yourself and want to cling onto what is safe and familiar, including the people around you, you slip so easily into the habit of pleasing others ahead of yourself.

As I am talking so much here about the impact difficult life-changing events can have on your life, I feel we must mention your responses to when things change unexpectedly around you also. People-pleasing is one such example.

When you disconnect from yourself and what you really want, you believe you need to be how others expect you to be. You convince yourself that it is the best way for you to keep everything the same and ensure that everyone remains happy with you. This most likely results in you saying 'yes' to going places and doing things when you want to say no; to being available to others when you should be looking after yourself; to agreeing with the general consensus rather than expressing your own opinions. You do everything to avoid upsetting the status quo.

AM I NOT BEING SELFISH?

One of the most common misconceptions when it comes to people-pleasing is that the opposite must mean you are selfish. But that's just it. The decision not to be a people pleaser doesn't actually mean you've decided you are *better* than anyone else, it is that you have chosen to believe that *you deserve better*.

Choosing to change your people-pleasing ways is you recognising the need to protect your own energy and space. It's you recognising that it's time to prioritise yourself and what you want, not continue to default to filling a never-ending void in the hope that others will never leave you.

Think about the people you know who have good boundaries and who are not prone to people-pleasing. Would you truthfully describe them as selfish? (Assuming that your definition of being selfish implies being mean and uncaring!). Or do you find yourself admiring their strength and confidence in being able to check in with themselves first before considering the demands of others?

YOU ONLY WANT TO BE LOVED

Let's be honest, you know how it feels to want people to like and accept you, to feel supported and heard. You have felt that urge, that desire, for the approval of others. It's natural and so it follows from this that there is nothing wrong with you wanting to be there for others to offer them help and support. But the real difficulty emerges when you lose yourself in the process of doing this.

You become so focused on being there for others, doing what they want and need, that you completely lose touch with what it is that **you** yourself might want or need. That's the official sign that you have moved into people-pleasing mode. You might even remember from earlier in this book that it's also evidence that you are disconnected.

Your life has become so much about the stories you live from, the patterns you keep recreating and the need to ensure that you are keeping everyone around you happy so that they will need you, love you and, at all costs, never abandon you. Most of you (myself most definitely included) become so distracted by the needs of others that you don't even notice that you no longer even know what yours are.

JOURNALING EXERCISE

I encourage you right now to take out a blank page and write out what it is you enjoy doing most and with who. This will help inform you what it is you should be doing *more* of and also what you might consider doing *less* of. When I first did this exercise, I began to see how often I was saying yes to the things I didn't want to do and that honestly surprised me.

Spending time thinking about these parts of yourself will also start to reveal what it is that matters most to you and that's an extremely powerful tool to have in your arsenal!

EXTERNAL VALIDATION

When you people-please, you begin to forget exactly who it is you are without other people, without their judgments, opinions or validation. You become so accustomed to seeking external validation that you choose to neglect who you are in favour of who it is you need to be.

You chase the approval and acceptance of others hoping that it will lead to an increase in your own feelings of self-worth. Spoiler: it doesn't. It's just you wanting to feel needed and worthy of love. You do everything possible to avoid that feeling of abandonment. You dim your light so that others can shine and you people-please.

ABANDON SHIP

Fear of abandonment is a significant issue in all of this. It absolutely was for me and, if I'm being honest, it still is. I've lost a lot of people in my life, mostly through circumstances beyond my control, but where it's relevant here is that it has altered how I show up in the world, and the relationships I continue to develop. The loss and absence of the people I care about has left me feeling fearful of losing more people.

If you're like me in this way, you may convince yourself that the more you can make yourself 'needed', the less likely it is that you will be abandoned again. I remember thinking that the more I did for others, the more grateful they would feel; and the kinder I was the more they would love me. I was wrong on both counts. It doesn't work that way.

If this sounds familiar to you then the chances are that the majority of decisions you've been making are also coming from a place of fear. Living like this is utterly exhausting – physically, mentally, emotionally and energetically. People-pleasing will do that to you. It leaves you feeling very depleted, deflated and, above all, empty.

Yet, you must also understand that people-pleasers often act the way they do because of these insecurities and their lack of self-esteem. For many, saying 'yes' becomes a natural habit. Not because it is right but because it is familiar.

THE 5 KINDS OF PEOPLE PLEASERS

Based on the significant amount of people I work with who closely identify with the act of people-pleasing, as well as the amount who want to change their people-pleasing ways, I created this system for my clients so that they can see themselves in one or more of these categories. It allows them to initially have some distance between these descriptions and their behaviour, and helps them view and understand themselves in a less critical way.

THE ORIGINAL (OG) – You all know them; you have all been them. They're the original people pleasers! These are the group who are just so damned nice and are tripping over themselves trying to keep everyone around them happy. They are the ones who constantly send messages into the group app so as not to leave anyone out. They spend hours inputting everyone's birthday into their phone (two days early so they can send the card). Their main purpose in life is to ensure everyone else happy.

THE SMOOTHIE – The one you want around when rows are breaking out! They want everyone to get along and smooth over any disagreements. If you're happy, they are happy. In a bid for them to feel safe and secure within their relationships, they work hard at making sure everyone around them is getting along harmoniously and feeling good!

THE GREAT PRETENDER – Also known as 'the denier', they come across as the tough, confident one. They are above it all and appear to have little interest in any definitions of people pleasers, often pretending to not even know what it means. However, they might in fact be avoiding having to confront the reality that this is their unique way of staying safe, and leading is the best way to avoid this. Apathy is their defence!

THE SUPPORT ACT – They dim their light so that someone else can shine. They see their supportive function as a deeply bonding exercise and they stand behind the centre of attention, making sure they have everything they need to maintain their place under the spotlight. They are the perfect Personal Assistant and take the role very seriously to ensure they prove themselves indispensable!

THE RECOVERING PEOPLE PLEASER - They have already

started to do the work around healing their people-pleasing behaviours in some shape or form. It's likely that they've had previous struggles with acting this at some stage in their life. Where once they might have made compromises around their time, energy and happiness to please others, as a Recovering People-Pleaser they've learnt (from hard-won experience) that this simply doesn't serve them.

Which one of these do you resonate most with? Please note that the objective of this is not to pigeonhole yourself or resign yourself to being one type or another, but for you to start observing how your people-pleasing ways show up in your life. Being aware of how you're doing this really helps when it comes to addressing what to do next to help you create greater balance in your life. Awareness is healing.

If you've no idea what type you are and would like help figuring it all out, then I've developed this quiz to help you decide which category you belong to: **www.niamhennis.com/quiz**. I love to hear what you think of the type you get, so please let me know how you get on!

SO, TELL ME, WHAT IS IT THAT YOU REALLY WANT?

Years back, when I started working with my first coach, I was stopped in my tracks when she asked me the simplest of questions. That same one I asked you earlier: '*What is it that you want? What really matters to you?*' I realised in that moment that, truthfully, I just didn't know. I genuinely hadn't a clue what it was that I wanted. I saw then that I had spent so long being informed by what others thought or what others expected for me that I no longer knew what it was that I – me, Niamh – wanted. I'd allowed myself to become so fully disconnected that I couldn't hear what my heart was screaming for.

WHAT IS YOUR HEART SCREAMING FOR?

To find your way back, you must reconnect with who you are and discover why it is perfectly okay for you to start saying no. In starting to say no, you are beginning to appreciate that it means you are saying yes to yourself. That can feel a little weird at the beginning and really takes some adjusting to. Perhaps, for the first time, you'll have to resist the notion that you're being selfish because you are now prioritising yourself.

This will require some deep diving so that you can begin to trust your friends will still be your friends, your family will still love you and your colleagues will still want to work with you, even if you can't always be there to help them out. You'll slowly learn that the right people will still respect you when you stand your ground or express an opinion that might be different to theirs.

Part of me will probably always want to be seen as the problem solver, the good girl, the one everyone gets along with. But the difference between then and now, is that my deep and personal understanding of who I am and everything that I choose to be and do, now flows from that place. I now know what it is that I want and exactly what matters to me. That's what I want for you too.

When you address your people-pleasing ways, you'll also acknowledge the disconnect inside of you. Remember earlier, we discussed how the way you treat yourself is linked directly to how you are inviting the world to treat you too. So, start now by setting the best possible example and put yourself first.

CLIENT CONVERSATIONS – JENNY

In many of our sessions, Jenny had talked in quite an animated fashion about her sister who 'could never miss a chance to take a swipe at my appearance when we were at family gatherings'. She found this relentless goading tiresome and also deeply hurtful. 'Why do you think this bothers you so much?' I asked her, in a bid to get her to start talking. 'Well, it's just another example of someone thinking it's okay to walk all over me.'

If I'm being honest I wasn't expecting that answer but, equally, it told me so much. It told me that there was more to this, much more. So I waited, gently prodding but waiting for whatever was to come next. What Jenny had not told me (until we were quite a way through our process) was that her husband had been having an affair for the best part of a year, and had done little to conceal it either. They had gone for couples counselling months ago, but it hadn't really helped.

Jenny distracted herself by keeping busy. 'I'm the one everyone asks when they need someone to run an errand or give a helping hand with something, or the friends who just want me to be there to listen as they dump their problems on me. It's what I've always done. Sometimes, if I'm being honest, I quite like that they need me but mostly I wish that they didn't.'

Together we explored what her own family situation had taught her about relationships, and she described a set-up where her dad was really good at pleasing himself. He didn't pay too much attention or in fact, care at all about pleasing anyone else. Her mum overcompensated and was fixated on just keeping the peace. She had wanted everyone to be happy and acted like she was oblivious to anything going wrong around her.

We each have different coping mechanisms and the reality is that no one way is the right or wrong way. They're each just different. But the foundations had been laid for Jenny from that time on to model her mum's way of doing things in her own marriage. She had allowed herself to replicate these people-pleasing ways and had allowed others to 'walk all over her'. Her sister, her friends and her husband all did what they did because she let them.

In our sessions, I encouraged Jenny to speak up about what it was **she** wanted and crucially what it was that she needed. We invested time getting clear on just what this was – how it looked and how it would feel to her.

We focused on helping her to say 'no' more often, starting with small things and working our way up. She describes this part as being 'very hard at the beginning. When it came to being available for everyone, I felt like I had to sit on my hands, bite my tongue, hide my phone, hide. I was overcome with guilt. I kept thinking, "I'm such a bad person. I'm so selfish doing this".'

We prepped her for quite a difficult conversation with her sister, which initially didn't go down too well, but was actually received better than Jenny thought it might be. 'My sister didn't like me pointing out that her comments were hurtful, but the truth is that she stopped slagging me off after we had that chat, so I consider that to be a positive result.'

Jenny shared what happened with her husband next. 'I gave my husband an ultimatum too and he left. That was the hardest part. I thought he'd love to see this new me emerge, but he was still too busy looking after himself. I'll be honest and say that I'm struggling with that piece, even now, mostly because it's totally out of my control, but I can absolutely see that it was never going to get any better. I needed to decide that I wasn't going to tolerate being made feel less than who I was.

'I'm left grieving for the life I thought we were going to have and need to work my way through that. Which I know I can now.

In addition, I definitely don't feel like it's quite so easy for people to walk over me now and that really makes me feel so much better about myself.'

THREE TIPS TO REDUCE YOUR PEOPLE-PLEASING WAYS

We'll explore the subject of creating boundaries in much greater depth in Chapter 12, but for now let's look at a few practical tips to help you reduce your people-pleasing ways:

TIP 1:

When a friend asks you to come shopping with her on Saturday morning, try not to give an answer to this question immediately. Learn how to buy time by using your new magic phrase, *'Let me get back to you on that'*. Previously, you'd have said 'yes sure!' and spent so much time afterwards agonising over it, asking *'why on earth did I say yes?'* Having bought yourself more time, you can then come up with a clear and measured response.

This response might in fact be the truth, which sounds like this: *'Saturday mornings are so precious to me. It's my one lie-in of the week. I cherish that time when I get to lie in bed reading and then take the dog out for a long walk. That's totally my time and I cherish it, so I'm going to say no, but be sure to send me photos of the outfits you're considering buying!'* Or you might want to go for the direct approach, which leaves little room for doubt: *'I have a long-standing coffee date on Saturdays with my mum/aunt/friend, so it has to be a no from me!'*

Just don't stray too far from the truth, it makes it easier to remember and is much more convincing!

TIP 2:

Imagine if someone at work asks you to help and you agree, despite being snowed under yourself, and then you immediately regret it. You're now angry, both at them *and* at yourself for saying 'yes' and you can really start to feel the resentment kicking in! Instead, why not say that you have to check your diary or to-do list, or check in with your partner first, and then you'll come back to them?

Do whatever you need to do to buy yourself some time. Then you'll have some extra space to think about it properly and can then respond later via text or email with a polite but firm 'no'. This isn't 'chickening out', but it does give you more time to make the right choice and not get talked around! Again, don't over-explain your reasons and don't backtrack on your decision either!

TIP 3:

Watch out for the toxic people in your life. They're the ones who push your boundaries because it benefits them and will make false promises like '*It won't be long*', '*just come for a little bit*', or '*you'll love it when you're there*'. I have a friend who I adore but she is especially skilful at getting you to say 'yes' when you really don't want to. I have learned to say '*I don't want to*' much more to her and, at the beginning, this made for some interesting lively exchanges, but now it's what she almost expects to hear!

THE POWER OF LANGUAGE

Take note of the language you are choosing to use as it can really influence their reactions.

'*I don't*' is much more powerful than '*I can't*'. It also shuts down toxic people faster. '*I don't*' establishes a clear and firm boundary, making you sound much more confident and clear in your intentions. Using '*I can't*' might seem like, and implies, that you're open to renegotiation. Try saying, '*I don't*': '*I don't want to go out for that birthday lunch. I don't have time to drop by tonight or I don't want to plan that far ahead. Let me come back to you closer to the time.*'

Be prepared for the fact that even those closest to you may not be equipped to deal with you suddenly saying '*no, I don't want to do that*'. Your changing changes the status quo and makes them feel a little unsafe in their own world. Be prepared for the inevitable pushback. It will come. It doesn't mean it's coming from a bad place, it's more likely coming from a place of fear, but it is likely that it will happen.

As you have been reading this, is there one specific person you have been thinking of? Someone who is constantly asking you to do things that you get sucked into doing despite not wanting to? Someone who you know, deep down, is in fact taking advantage of you but you're simply too scared to say 'no' to?

Don't worry if there is; you're not alone. We all have that 'someone' in our lives, but we don't always admit to it or are not always able to see them for who they are. We don't always feel strong enough to stop them from doing it, which is why this work is so vital.

Do more of what makes you feel good, with *who* makes you feel good

The very best way to alter your people-pleasing ways is to focus more on doing what makes you feel good. If you feel good, you won't need others so much to make you feel good. Imagine how that would make you feel.

Ask yourself what sparks joy in your life throughout the day. Take a note of it. You want to gather as many of these events, incidents and occasions so you can then continue to replicate them and create more of just what makes you feel good. When you feel good, you are less likely to feel the urge to people-please; you'll feel more confident and able to speak up to ask for exactly what you want.

Avoid putting yourself in the company of people who for whatever reason leave you feeling depleted and drained. Steer clear of those who thrive on gossiping and negativity; spend more time with those who make you feel better about and in yourself without you having to do anything for them. Think of the people in your life that you can fully be yourself with. That's where you want to be.

When you have much greater clarity on what it is you want to do with your life and who you want to do it with, you're much more willing to ask for it because you believe you deserve it. Look around you and observe that that's what most other happy people are doing anyhow.

FEEL THE FEELINGS

When it comes to people-pleasing, successes and disappointments (*note: there are no failures*) you'll have to use your feelings as a guide. It's simply a case of arriving at what feels right to you now at this moment and then deciding what you are willing to do about it.

But also, remember that when you are disconnected being able to hear and pay attention to these feelings can be a real challenge. The more you continue people-pleasing, the more you are reinforcing that disconnection from your heart. What happens when you address this and focus on changing your people-pleasing ways, is that you ultimately reactivate your heart space, making yourself familiar with your feelings again and paving the way for real and lasting change.

GO WITHIN

Fall back on your daily practice of journaling, affirmations and meditating. Be compassionate with yourself. This is you going cold turkey. You are aiming to break the habits of a lifetime, so be patient and above all be kind to yourself when doing this!

THOUGHTFUL TOOLS

- If you said no when you meant no, how would your life be different?

- Why does putting yourself first feel so wrong? Why do you think this is? What two things could you do now that would begin to address this?

- Describe a recent situation where you felt really good about yourself.

- What were you doing? Who was there?

- What was it about this situation that made you feel so good?

- How can you do more of this?

- Think about a time when you said what you felt and did what you wanted to. How did it feel?

CHAPTER 7

TOUGH-LOVE ENERGY

It is never what happens externally that decides what light we allow into our hearts, but rather the decisions we make internally that will reveal our choices.

Maybe after processing some of the clear signs that you are disconnected, you're feeling a little drained. Perhaps you've identified easily with all three: comparison, dimming to fit in and people-pleasing. Possibly you are, for the first time, understanding why you are the way you are and why you feel the way you feel. Maybe also, you don't quite recognise this new feeling that you're now feeling. Well, let me reassure you, this is what being heard feels like.

My reason for talking about these three signs and for sharing these client conversations was exactly that: I want you to feel heard. I want you to know that, despite how it might look on the outside, so many of you are going through your own private and personal upheavals. You all work hard at trying to appear like everything is running smoothly, not to deceive or mislead, but because it's how you've been told how to do it. But remember, that when your internal voice is telling you that everyone else has it so much better than you, the chances are very high that they don't.

I also wish to share with you my firm belief that nobody should have to do this business of life alone. Think back to the times when community was everything; yet look at how, in today's world, that's changing all around us. You were never meant to function in isolation, but somewhere along the way you absorbed the belief that you were. You listened to that story that told you asking for help implied weakness, and that opting to do everything yourself demonstrated independence, and so you continued believing that you must do it all on your own.

WHO ARE YOU NOW THAT YOUR LIFE HAS CHANGED?

When you experience hard times, you end up doing everything you can, pulling on all your resources to recreate the life you had before everything changed. *You want to go back to being the person you were before this all happened.*

You think that's where the answer lies. You assume that by trying to get back to that place you will be able to feel how you felt before this happened. But that's not the reality, is it? Something has changed, something big. Perhaps someone is no longer in our lives, or your circumstances have altered dramatically; whatever it is, it means that you now need to change with it.

When someone close to you leaves or dies, or a friendship ends, you would give anything to be back with that person, to feel like you did before they left. You run through all the 'what ifs' and regrets. You convince yourself that the answer to this pain and disappointment is simply to go back to feeling how you felt before.

Your life becomes split in two – the before and the after. This happens whether it be the loss of a relationship or a job, a loved one or your sense of self, you're constantly reliving the past and wishing the present away. It applies to any and all life-changing events. You fondly remember the before and you carefully avoid the after.

Your life has changed and part of accepting loss of any kind is accepting that change. It's a very human reflex to want to be able to see past the pain, to want to get beyond it. Before or after. Anywhere other than here in the depths of your pain. Little by little, you'll learn to integrate the pain of that loss. Who you were before it happened is never the same as who you are now? And you know what, that's okay.

'If I don't have my past and I can't visualise my future,
then who on earth am I?'

This speaks to my own personal experience. It was grief in its full rawness as I tried to settle into my new place in the world, without that person who had died or left. My identity had taken such a battering and yet I was expected to continue living and stepping into a life that no longer felt safe or in any way familiar.

It's why I also felt the need to consider a different life, not because I was running away (*although let's face it, that's exactly what I wanted to do*), but because I needed to create a different space so that I could breathe again, be myself again, and not have the reminders of everything I had lost or reminders of everyone who was missing.

Pain disconnects you

For my part, it took at least five years before I could feel the scar forming over the wound of my first bereavement. That's a long time to be in pain. But when I say '*forming*', I have to tell you that it fell off a few times, which is my clumsy way of saying that you never get over something like this. You never accept it. You never feel ready to move on with your life. And that's okay. You take a step forward, something pulls you back, you stand still, you go again and on and on it goes.

Things slowly changed for me when I could begin to accept that the life I had before loss was gone. The person I was before was also gone. What remained was somewhat a shell of a woman, but a woman with a beating heart, an active mind and a determination to do something with her life. At that time that was all I needed to know.

Who was I without grief? Answer: I was Mrs Angry

But as the scar was forming and I was feeling more able to immerse myself back into the real world, I saw that something else was at play. I slowly started to see that I had in fact become a little addicted to the sympathy.

I'd been in pain for so long that the truth was, I didn't know who I was without it. Over the following months, as I tried to locate the answers, I saw something else that I had been hiding behind – I had become angry, resentful, jealous and even a little bitter.

I knew anger was a sign of grief, but I wasn't simply angry about the loss, I was angry with everyone and everything else. I was resentful that here I was, in my thirties, very alone with no clue where I was going to go next or what I should do if I got there. I was angry that, not for the first time, I was the odd one out. I was so tired of being the one who got bad stuff thrown at her repeatedly.

I was totally fed up with being the person that bad things happened to. I was angry, but I wasn't fired up about it. That was the thing. I felt flattened by it. It had become my norm. It was just how things were. It was the story I had allowed to envelop me.

Being 'poor Niamh' was the easiest way out of it. If people felt sorry for me, I wouldn't have to change. I could stay here. So, I did.

WHAT IF THIS WAS MY LOT?

Sitting at home on my couch one evening, a thought came to me that perhaps I needed 'to accept the fact that I was someone who bad things just happened to'; maybe this wasn't the lifetime where I'd attract good things and that this would happen in the next one. I can honestly remember every word of this internal conversation.

Even at that time, it didn't feel overly dramatic (though I can see now that it was), it felt like a sensible and logical way for me to think at that time. It made complete sense in that moment. With the benefit of hindsight, however, I can see that this was me in full-on *victim mode*. Having already disconnected from myself, I was now declaring that nobody could help me, that I didn't need anyone else and that it was best all-around that I accept that this was my lot.

But while I can somewhat smile recalling this, I can also remember the dark place I was in at that time. I'd not only disconnected from myself, I had fully detached from myself.

You are never abandoned – you only ever abandon yourself

Three things you might not want to hear but you need to

I'll never stop saying this, but this is not directed at anyone in the early stages of recovering from a life-changing event. This applies only to those who have allowed themselves to go through the difficult first few months and even years. This is for those of you who deep down know you are ready to rebuild their lives but just don't feel able to start. Some of this might feel harsh if you're not ready to hear it, or even if you are ready.

In order for you to grow, you must release; in order for you to heal, you must face the pain; and in order for you to feel empowered and stronger, you must stop your refusal to acknowledge your part in all of this. Deep down you know it can't be all everyone else's fault. But to accept that you played a part or still play a part in this is to admit that the solution rests with you too!

1. ACCEPT RESPONSIBILITY.

Let's be honest, when anything goes wrong in any area of your life, it's so much easier for you to ask *'whose fault is this?'* Someone must be to blame for this. Someone. Anyone, but you.

By abdicating all responsibility, you revert to that child-like feeling of *'it wasn't me, it was them'*. It can be a hard truth to recognise and accept that while you might not be to blame for ending up in these difficult situations, you are always responsible for how long you stay there.

I know that might not go down too well with everyone, but you truly can't continue to allow events from your past to govern or determine your future. You must search for a way to relinquish your need to blame others and accept that it is now your time to do something about it. Yes, life is hard, yes, it's unfair that you feel you're having to manage more bad things than others, but no, a big fat no, to anyone else being responsible for how you let this play out in your future life. That is within your control to change.

Signs you're blaming others

It's important that you can recognise when you are doing this. I recall when I started to observe myself saying or thinking that where I was in my life and what had happened to me was all because of something that someone else did. I got very used to pointing the finger outward. I did this because it was easier for me to believe that if someone else caused me pain in the past then they were somehow responsible for everything that was to happen in my future. In blaming others, I gave myself permission to continue to wallow in my pain.

Whether you're beginning to realise that nobody likes to hang out with a 'Debbie Downer' or you can see that your behaviour is starting to cause concern for others, you do know that no one is going to swoop in and clear away your problems for you? You alone have to do the work.

You know how in your own story you're the main character, you get to create the plot, plan the dialogue and dress yourself in your favourite outfit? Well, in everyone else's you're the secondary one, saying what they think you would say, doing what they expect of you and wearing that horrible outfit because they really don't care!

Do you accept that nobody thinks about your problems or your life quite as much or certainly not to the level that you do? They've got their own lives, their own challenges and their own worries. They can want you to be happy again, but also want to get on with living their own lives. They saw when you were struggling, and they felt your pain. They were there for you. They supported you in every way possible. But the thing is, they can't always be there for you. They can't take away your pain. They can support you, but they too need to see that you are willing and prepared to support yourself.

That familiar place, where you feel most comfortable is also known as the home of self-pity. It's debilitating and draining, not just for you but for others too. The further you sink into that energetic space the more you attract it into your life. Misery loves company. I know it's hard to hear this. I know, because I remember when I needed to be told this too. You can slip into victimhood too easily, often without you even being aware of it, and have it serve as a cloak to protect you from any more harm. You think if you play the victim you won't have to deal with the reality of your circumstances.

It's such a big step for you to decide that you might just be ready to take full responsibility for what happens in your life next. That's when you declare it is time for you to enter fully into the next phase of your life, changed and different but much more willing to assume responsibility for who it is you are becoming.

CLIENT CONVERSATIONS – MARIANNE

Our tendency to not always accept responsibility is not a new one. Going right back to the very beginning when Adam and Eve were caught in the first act of sin, what did they do? They pointed the finger at someone else! How many times have we heard or used 'it wasn't me, it was her!' It's so much easier to convince ourselves and others that something else is to blame, someone else is at fault and to abdicate all our own sense of personal responsibility.

When Marianne came to work with me there was a lot happening in her life. She was having trouble at work and her partner had recently told her she didn't think things were working out and that perhaps they should consider taking a break. She didn't know what to do and was desperate for some guidance. There was a sense of urgency about Marianne like she wanted everything fixed now. Her energy felt chaotic, but you couldn't miss the fear in her eyes.

When someone presents a situation where there are two areas causing them concern, I immediately look for the link. Something out of whack in one area will very often show up in another area.

When I got her to talk about work, it appeared that the problem lay with her manager. 'She keeps putting more and more work my way and it's just not fair. No one else seems to have the volume of cases to get through that I have! It's like she has it out for me, but I daren't say anything as my annual review is coming up!'

It's not helped by what's going on at home. 'I don't understand why my partner Angie is suddenly saying things aren't working out. Yes, alright, it hasn't been the easiest of years, I lost my Mum at the end of last year, but I'm doing the best I can with what I have. I wish she could be a little more understanding!'

There it was. Her manager is overloading her and her partner is being unreasonable. **And her mother died.**

Her mother dying had set off a spiral of events in her life, and in her grief, she had become quite angry with everyone around her. She was blaming her manager, who most likely was trying to keep her busy at work by giving her plenty to do. She knew just how capable she was and she also knew that when her dad died a few years earlier work had been a great refuge.

Angie had in truth carried the brunt. As is often the case, you hurt those closest to you because it's easiest. Unable to articulate her grief because it would make it even more real, she had disconnected and closed down a part of her that would have allowed her to speak to Angie about how lost and sad she felt. Instead, she was angry, angry that her mum had gone and angry that nobody seemed to really care.

For months now she had lashed out at everyone and everything, and the carefree Marianne was no longer anywhere to be seen. While in our sessions, she and I could now understand why she was doing this and we could now explain what was behind it, but we could not begin to address it until Marianne started to accept responsibility for her own actions.

You blame other people because it means you don't have to deal with what's happening right in front of you. You find it easier to hold other people responsible for how you are feeling because it stops you from having to. Blaming others is a form of denial but mostly is also a form of survival.

No, she wasn't responsible for her mother's death and yes, she needed as much time and space to grieve as was necessary, but she also needed to see that everyone in her life was just doing their best and by shutting them out and being angry with them, blaming them, she was creating a whole set of new challenges to deal with.

She needed to sit down with Angie, as she had done with me, and explain just how hard she was finding this entire situation. She needed to apologise for any time she had not been there in their relationship and hope that Angie could see that she was being sincere. She was hurting.

With regards to her manager at work, she didn't say anything, but being more aware of her actions caused her to change her demeanour and over the following weeks and months things really felt like they were improving. At her review, which actually went well, she made a point to thank her manager for her support.

Marianne and Angie are continuing to work on things but accepting responsibility and not blaming others for how she was feeling has gone such a long way to improving communications. Each week now they sit down and have a little check-in on how they are both feeling, which is helping them both a lot.

Marianne's story points to the belief that you can't control everything in your life. Bad things happen but you can absolutely control the choices you make. You can control how you react and who your actions and behaviours impact. Life is often painful and deeply unfair, but that doesn't give you permission to do whatever you want in response. You are still responsible for your actions, for all that you say and for how you treat others.

When you own your mistakes and accept responsibility, it also has the potential to bring much joy into your life as you heal broken relationships and seek forgiveness and understanding from those you may have blamed along the way.

2. DETACH FROM THE DRAMA

You can, of course, stay where you are. You have the perfect reason, after all, for feeling bad. Nobody would really blame you. You can totally defend your choice to be as you are, to feel as you feel. Or you could open yourself up to stretching yourself, pushing yourself even when it doesn't feel comfortable, even when you want to run back to your familiar hideout. You could confess to having become so used to people offering to do things for you, to help you, to listen to you, to feel sorry for you. You could admit that you have become attached to their sympathy.

Do you really want to do what I did and keep wallowing, to stay attached to the drama in your life? Do you want to immerse yourself so deeply into the sad times of your life that they become your current times?

Or, are you past that point where you need and want to detach yourself from the drama and dip your toe back into life and live once more? You could let that mask slip and allow people to see that you aren't the resilient warrior woman you've convinced them you are. You could show them that how you've been living since this awful thing happened to you is not life and how you are finally ready to detach from the drama. Just because those stories might have been true once, hell, they might even be true today, but it doesn't mean that they need to be true for you in your future. You're done with them.

CLIENT CONVERSATIONS – MYSELF!

When I lived through my own experiences of grief and because they came in quick succession, I bounced around a lot and at times I'll be honest I wasn't even sure who it was on any given day I was grieving for. It became a bit of a mishmash in my head and this confusion contributed to my feeling of helplessness.

I had an incredible network around me of strong women who kept me pointed in the right direction. When they'd see me start to turn around, they would gently catch me by my elbow and ease me back on track. Caitriona was one of these women and while it's never good to single out just one person, she was always the one I could be most honest with.

She would tell me repeatedly that while she didn't understand what I was going through, she was always there to listen. What makes Caitriona such a treasured friend is that she held space for me but didn't pander to me. I needed that. She would patiently repeat the story of that very last time when she drove me to the hospital to be with Tony as he died, because she knew just how scared I was that I might forget even one little detail.

The times I started to see a life beyond my grief were always when I was with her. She was the first person that got me talking, thinking and even laughing about something that didn't involve me. We would discuss other things for a while and then eventually I'd bring it back to me. She allowed me to do this. I was able to laugh my head off and not be worried that it might be seen as disrespectful or inappropriate. I could just as quickly do my big ugly cry and regularly did, but I never once felt I couldn't say anything or do anything differently when she was there versus when I was on my own. That's the very best gift a friend can give when you are grieving.

So, it was no surprise when she and I were talking one day that I admitted I was troubled by something – 'I'm worried I'm milking this.' I had genuinely become so attached to the drama of all of it that I was concerned I might be starting to exploit it. The thing is that there was some truth in that. I knew something bad had happened. I'd lost those closest to me, that was a fact. That was the truth, but how I was living with it three maybe four years later was not necessarily healthy. I had gotten so used to people giving me the sad head tilt, had become so accustomed to people making allowances for me, that I felt I was on the cusp of taking advantage of it. And I was.

Of course, Caitriona didn't necessarily agree with that, she wanted to point out that I had good reason to feel how I did, but notwithstanding this, she did encourage me to start looking for ways to manage things that might make me feel better about myself.

That was the beginning of me detaching myself from the drama and looking for ways to do things differently so that I might start to feel differently. It was also the first time I felt able to rely on my own judgement and reconnect with that sense of independence that had been such a source of strength to me before all this had happened.

I had felt safe doing this with Caitriona and will remain eternally grateful for the love and support she so readily gave to me at a time when I needed it most. It helped me more than she will ever know and more than I will ever be able to express to her.

Detaching from your drama requires real courage. Don't assume it will feel easy, it won't, but trust that you need to do this so that you can be reminded of how your life was before all of this happened. This is what moving from pain to power feels like. It feels sticky, uncomfortable, messy, unpleasant and unbearable, let's not sugar coat it, but the alternative is that you remain stuck where you are and trust me you don't want that. You want to feel strong and powerful, and you will. Soon.

Just think about the level of authority you have over what happens to you. These aren't glib words on a page. These are facts. You get to move yourself from that place of pain to a place of power. But you must choose to do it.

3. FIND THE COURAGE YOU NEED

Fear is a reaction and courage is a decision. To reclaim your power you need to *decide* to be courageous and brave. Your world as you had come to know it has changed and you have been asked to change with it. Not only are you unsure how to, you aren't even sure you want to, but to keep moving forward you must choose to.

Irish writer, Emma Donoghue in her 2010 book called *Room* encapsulates this stage so beautifully: '*scared is what you're feeling, brave is what you're doing.*'

Trust me, I know that you will look back and remember this time and how hard it was in all its detail. But staying put and reliving your pain is no longer a choice for you.

However, I want you to remember that you are *not* dishonouring anything or anyone from your past by choosing to let go. Nor are you being selfish by wishing for your feelings to change. You are simply doing your best given who you are now with what you are left with.

You will feel guilty. You'll feel it's too soon and that you're not being appropriate, that you won't meet others' expectations. You'll feel all of those things. But that doesn't make any of them true. You have no idea just how this story will end, you actually don't need to, but you are deciding to change direction regardless, which right now shows me just how courageous you are being. When you tune into your courage you can achieve most things.

CLIENT CONVERSATIONS – TILLY

Tilly was another client who came to me because she was genuinely miserable in her job, but she could see no way out. In truth, there weren't an enormous number of options available to her, for reasons we will explain later.

Five years ago, Tilly had secured her dream job. It was with a very high-profile investment bank that had a great reputation for training up their graduates. The first four years had been great. In fact, everything in her life had been great. She'd enjoyed incredible holidays, had had a great group of girlfriends, had married her childhood sweetheart Tom, and they'd bought their first home. She was finding her work interesting and felt like she was constantly learning and growing in her role in a way that excited her for what was to come.

There was quite a bit of talk that she was ready to step into a management role and if she was being honest, she felt ready for it. She wasn't cocky but felt confident. Her reviews had all been excellent and her manager had told her that she would be recommending her when the time came. When she heard earlier this year that they were planning a restructure, she couldn't help but think that this was her time.

Her manager had been true to her word, but in fact, she herself was amongst one of the first casualties in what turned out to be a cost-cutting exercise, as several departments were culled and merged at the same time.

As if that wasn't bad enough, it quickly became apparent that in her new manager, Tilly was discovering someone less concerned with a happy work environment and more obsessed with efficiencies. Everything changed for her in that year. Her workload doubled, her salary was frozen and all talk of progression and promotion was shelved. She felt she couldn't *say anything at work because so many had been let go and she felt guilty for even voicing it, but she was miserable and for the first time she hated going to work each morning.*

At the same time, something else happened. Her husband Tom lost his job unexpectedly. So here was Tilly now, in a job that she had hated that was quite literally sucking the life out of her, and the fact that Tom was now out of work, she knew meant she could do nothing. She had to stay. There were no other options available to her.

The situation at work worsened and her relationship with her manager deteriorated. It was around this time that she came to one of my Time for Change workshops. We started working together shortly after on a 1-1 basis, and my first task was to rebuild her. I sensed she had allowed herself to lose all hope and I could see some resentment starting to kick in! 'I know Tom's situation won't be forever, but I wish I didn't have to carry the can all by myself.' She was also starting to take how her manager was behaving almost too personally, convinced that he had it out for her. The truth was it sounded like he was doing a difficult job in a tough situation, but she didn't want to see that.

So where was her way out? Well, it had to start with her reclaiming her power. She needed to see that there was light at the end of the tunnel. And to do that she must be the one to create it. We spent a lot of time working on what it was that she really wanted to do. I asked her, 'In an ideal world, if you had no fears or money worries what would you do?' and got her to really think about her answer, which was: 'I'd find the courage to stop moping and go out and do something instead!'

Over the next six months, this is exactly what we did. We got busy identifying an area that she had a huge passion for. We carried out lots of research around it, including finding out what upskilling and qualifications she might need. Tilly also put time aside first thing every morning to look after her mindset during which she journaled and used affirmations. Together we created a realistic schedule for her to get from where she was to where she wanted to go. We identified two people working in this area she really admired and set up meetings for her with them. This was such a valuable exercise for her as it really clarified for her what it was she needed to do but, more importantly, what it was she wanted to do.

We prepared a budget that would allow her to meet her current financial responsibilities but would leave her able to afford her extra training. She wisely invested some of her spare time helping Tom get his name back out there and made sure they still remembered to have fun during this stressful time.

It wasn't easy. She continued to experience wobbles along the way, but the one thing she says really helped her was, 'having a plan, being able to visualise a way out. Once I saw that, I didn't feel so helpless about where I was. You gave me back my power and realising that all of that was in my hands made all the difference'.

TOUGH-LOVE ENERGY QUESTIONS

- Are you ready now to accept responsibility for what happens next in your life?

- Can you concede that you've got very used to the sympathy and have, in fact, begun to depend on it?

- Are you prepared to acknowledge and detach from your drama?

- Do you recognise that you've relinquished all your power and are letting past events determine what happens in your future?

If you answered 'yes' to all but the last question, then you are game and it's time. You are ready to move on to the next part of this book where I will share with you what you need to do to move you from there to here. From pain to power.

To release what's not serving you. To stop you from living a story that is no longer appropriate and assist you in rewriting a new one. To release your attachment to the sympathy and the drama. To live again without leaving behind what you have learned or who you have lost.

THOUGHTFUL TOOLS

Before we dive into Part Two and look at the ways you are going to embrace these changes, I want you to stop now and make the ultimate promise, which is the one to yourself to do this, to do what's needed, to face the messy bits, acknowledge the cringe-worthy bits and to confront the challenging bits.

COMMITMENT EXERCISE

I, {Niamh Ennis}, declare that from this day forward, I accept full responsibility for the rest of my life. I am done blaming everyone else for how I am feeling. I am finished relying on their sympathy. I withdraw my addiction to drama. I acknowledge that in trying to protect myself I have closed myself off to change. I accept I have become disconnected from myself. I admit that I am living from a story that is out of date and is not even altogether mine.

Well, no more.

Today, I commit to doing all that I need to so that I can be more of who I want to become. I choose to celebrate the success of others and trust that when my time comes, I will be excited and ready. I open myself up to what's coming next. I believe that things are always working out for me.

PART TWO

CHAPTER 8

CLARITY, VISION & VALUES

In Part One we explored where you may have disconnected and where you still might be. Next, I plan to focus in on the steps that will reunite your head and your heart.

To be fair, unless you have quite a clear and detailed vision of where you want to go, how on earth can you expect to get there? You don't jump in your car, turn the engine on and scream at the car to take you to where it thinks you might want to go. Well, at least I hope you don't. Instead, you most likely have a definite image in mind of your end destination, how to get there, the towns, motorways, landmarks to look out for along the way, as well as how long it should take and what you need to bring with you for the journey. All of this gives you the confidence to trust that if you stick to your planned route, you'll get eventually get there.

In Part Two, we will get you closer to identifying and creating that vision of your end destination.

- What does it look like? Give as much detail here as possible.
- What do you *want* it to look like? Imagine yourself getting there.
- What will you *feel* like when you get there?

But that's not all. Once you can visualise it I'll start furnishing you with all the appropriate tools so that you can activate it in your mind and bring it to life with ease. You are done with thinking and talking about this. No more '*what ifs*' or '*I'll do it whens*'. You are now entering the 'doing' mode!

CLARITY

First things first. As we have already alluded to, when you are about to embark on any journey you want to know first where you are going so that you can recognise it when you get there. That's exactly why I'd like us to start here, to help you get greater clarity on what you want to achieve and where exactly you want to go; for you to recognise just what needs to change for you to reach your end destination.

Getting clarity is not just about naming your goals, it goes much deeper than that. It involves you being really clear on exactly what you want from your life. You get clarity by asking questions of yourself often for the first time, so be sure to give yourself space and time to listen for the answers.

The relationship between change and clarity is very powerful. When you obtain greater clarity, you move yourself closer towards implementing real change and transformation. You place yourself in a much stronger position to connect with that part of you that wants something new, something better, which is what we are going to do for you in the following chapters.

But first, you promised...

At the end of the first part of this book, you declared (to the only person who mattered, yourself) that you were ready to accept responsibility and do what you needed to do to move you forward. You committed to reconnecting and rewriting your story. Did you really mean it? Well, you're about to find out.

We all know that you can use words to deflect attention. You can use them so that others will stop asking you if you have done something or if you want something. But the one person you can't fob off or push away is you. The truth always catches up on you and even the act of disconnecting in order to protect yourself works only for a while.

Focus on your vision

There are many components that together will constitute your personal vision for the future. The story you live by, the values you hold, who it is you want to become, your ability to express yourself and how you aspire to show up in the world through connecting with your purpose.

What unites all of these is determined by how living out your vision makes you feel. That's the measure. That's the gauge. How does it make you feel now, knowing that you are on the way to making it real?

When you believe that something is possible, doors begin opening. What you once thought impossible now becomes possible. What you once thought unlikely now takes a form known to you. Serendipitous opportunities appear when you believe. When you see it, you can be it, that bit is true; but how can you become something if you have no concept of what it looks like? Even if it's a dream. Especially if it's a dream.

Often, when I suggest to clients that they must trust the signs, I see their eyes raise ever so slightly. I get that for some talking about trusting the signs might be a step too far, but I truly believe there are signs all around you that you can only see if you are open to them. You meet someone who turns out to be the right person to help you at the right time, you hear a discussion on a subject you are wrestling with, or you ask for help from the universe and a feather, a robin or a deer will appear before you.

Try looking out for your signs and you may be surprised. Better still, why not ask for a sign? But if you do, be prepared to see it.

THE TOOLS

Intention setting

Setting intentions is when you declare exactly what it is you plan on achieving through your deliberate actions. It's when you commit to what you want the journey to entail as you proceed. When you are intentional about something your focus is very much in the present. When you are intentional, you choose to make decisions and take action based on what's really important to you. Being intentional means getting clear from the outset about what it is you want to achieve.

Before you embark on any activity, it's important that you set a clear intention in your mind and preferably commit it to paper. Be sure it tells you what your desired outcome is, why you want it so much, how you will feel when you get there and exactly what it is you want from this.

Setting your intention also has the added benefit of keeping you focused on what it is you are working towards. It's far easier to stay on track when you know **why** something matters to you. Connecting with your 'why' reinforces your existing intention. When you have that clear vision of who you want to be and the reason it matters so much to you, then you have your why.

It's *why* you're doing it, *why* you want change, *why* you want to get unstuck, *why* you want to rebuild your life. It's also why you deserve it. So why not have a strong, vivid image in your mind that you can return to, which will really bring it to life for you when setting your intention?

Your values – what matters most to you right now?

I was lucky enough to have had parents who had very strong values and were incredibly attached to them. My dad had this deep innate sense of justice that served as his moral compass. He was incredibly certain as to what he should do or say in any given situation, and it was one of the qualities I loved and admired about him the most. He taught me so much about how to treat people, especially the underdog, as well as what friendship should look like and the importance of respecting yourself enough to always stand up for what you believe in.

Unsurprisingly, these values were instilled in me from an early age, and I have always been incredibly aware of the difference between doing what's right and doing what's wrong. In the interest of full transparency, I won't pretend that I always do the right thing, but I always know what it is. I'm a work in progress and aspiring to be more like my dad every day in every way.

Let me ask you this: if someone were to question you

today on what your values are, would you know? Would you perhaps default to your understanding of values or would you connect with that inner knowing of *'what matters most to you'* right now?

During the recent global pandemic, people witnessed their values shifting radically. They found that when forced to slow down what mattered most to them was spending quality time with themselves and their families, getting out and really reconnecting with nature, doing more of what they loved and prioritising their own needs first.

So, do you know what your current values are? I say current because your values should evolve as you evolve. Think in terms of the different areas of your life – you, your family, your career, your relationships, your health and your friendships. You can expect that what matters to you right now may not have mattered to you before when you were younger, or most likely won't in your future either.

The world is moving at such a pace that your values are changing with greater speed than ever, so it's prudent that you keep checking in to refresh what these values are.

Why values matter

When you are sure of your values you will find it so much easier to make decisions, because you will be doing so now from a greater place of alignment. The next time you are asked to make a decision or a choice, check in with yourself and ask: *'does this really feel in line with my values and will it get me closer to them?'* Your decision will be there in the answer!

Imagine a job opportunity arises and you wonder if it's for you. You then measure it against your values and question, *'will taking this job help you get closer to achieving what matters most to you right now?'* Or indeed, if you're wondering about a relationship and whether it is good for you, measure it against your values and ask the same question. This is the gift that knowing what truly matters to you brings you, and your decision-making gets a little easier.

If you find this a little challenging at first, then simply focus on what matters most, not what needs to be prioritised or requires urgent attention; think about what actually matters most to you? When you train yourself to consider what feels best for you and not what you have been told you should want, think or do, your decisions will feel less conflicting and more natural, which is exactly what real clarity feels like.

Your best next step

Armed with these new tools, you can now see exactly where you are going and what route you need to take to end up where you want. You possess a clear understanding of what matters most to you right now; you know the best next steps that will get you there. Next, we want you to work on giving yourself the permission to make that change, which we will look at in more depth in the following chapter.

You know that it won't always feel comfortable and there will be speed bumps on the way, but because this matters, change matters, you'll keep going. You are aware that *'vision without action is just a dream'*, so this is your call to stop thinking about it, stop hiding and take action. When you get there, I promise you won't look back and ask why you did it; you'll most likely ask *'why did it take me so long to take that first step?'*

The image is forming now of the woman you want to become. You're getting closer to uncovering exactly who she is and how you will feel being her. But in recognising it, you're one step closer to acknowledging that you alone have the power to change all of that. If you choose it.

We have already discovered that giving yourself permission means accepting that the responsibility for this happening lies with you. The real question is, are you ready for that now? How can you not be?

Where feels like home?

As you begin to describe and have a greater understanding of where it is you want to get to, I'd encourage you to think about where feels most like home to you? I believe that you find home where you find yourself. It's inside you, but it emerges only when you feel fully safe and free to be yourself in all situations, amongst all people or none.

I struggled for the longest time with this and had no sense of where it was that I belonged. I honestly didn't feel like I belonged anywhere. I waited for that feeling that would indicate I had found my place, but it never came.

I was quick to believe the old stories and blamed myself for not being enough or often for being too much. It wasn't until I found myself questioning the truth of this narrative that I heard myself ask, 'what if you weren't meant to belong?' I remember that moment as being a real turning point, as I finally released the pressure to belong. I found freedom in letting go of the belief that I had to belong somewhere else when I already belonged to myself.

Once I started to dance with the idea that perhaps all along I had been chasing the wrong star and that my life's objective did not need to be about being accepted, but rather to accept myself instead, things started to feel lighter.

I would dearly love to have had this conversation with my fourteen-year-old self! I would have told her that doing whatever was required to fit in would almost guarantee remaining on the outside and that obsessing about belonging would only distract me from what really needed my attention. I could have saved her from the years of angst and disappointment she endured for never really feeling at home; if only I had realised that I didn't need to be accepted. I just needed to accept myself.

It can be too easy to look for solutions outside of yourself when really the answer is always inside you. This is what happens when you disconnect from yourself, when you attach yourself to a false narrative and have no real vision of who you are before you can even contemplate who it is you want to become.

CLIENT CONVERSATIONS – LISA

Coming home doesn't mean moving home and it took Lisa quite a while to recognise that. She had had the travel bug for as long as she remembered. She had been to all of the usual spots: Australia, New Zealand Bali, Vietnam, Cambodia, Canada, Cuba, Brazil, Peru and much of Europe. She felt very fortunate to live in an age not just where travel was possible but where updating her tens of thousands of followers on Instagram as she went made sponsorship and income generation possible, and had somehow turned this into a career for herself. At 29, she certainly knew how to pack a backpack! There was so much of this lifestyle that she loved and this was enough to quieten the sensible part of her brain that would ask her what her long-term plan was!

Then we entered a global pandemic and everything changed. It was during this period that she and I started working together. She thought this forced time at home would be the perfect time 'to sort out her life stuff!'

From the beginning, I could see that Lisa approached her life like she did her backpack. Everything had a pocket and belonged somewhere. Her ability to compartmentalise was admirable, but it was also stopping her from looking at the bigger picture. She had no strategy and no plan other than navigating what was right in front of her. This served her well for all of her travel endeavours, but she was starting to understand that it might not be the solution for everything else.

I began by asking her to describe what she loved about her life (there was a lot), and then what she would like to change or to have more of. What was most interesting was that she genuinely struggled when asked to dive deep. Not in a 'holding your cards close to your chest' kind of way but in that she was *totally unable to articulate anything that came close to sharing feelings.*

It wasn't because she was nervous or afraid of sharing, but because this was something she had never done before. Ever. She suspected she might have been a little guarded, but she hadn't realised just how closed she was. This genuinely surprised and alarmed her. On closer inspection, it emerged that Lisa was deeply uncomfortable once we moved past the artificial stuff. By her own admission, her discomfort led her to shut people out and keep them at arm's length. Her nomadic lifestyle enabled this. It was easier not to divulge too much of herself for safety reasons, but also it meant she didn't get too attached.

Through a series of journaling exercises to help Lisa identify where this might have started, the answer revealed itself. When she was just eleven years of age, her friend and cousin Jean drowned in a freak accident. While her parents had tried their best and protected her from knowing too much detail about it all, her memory was that one day Jean was there and the next she wasn't. She remembers missing her cousin so much but also not being able to talk to anyone about it as she didn't want to upset them. She did what she thought they wanted her to do. She acted as if nothing had happened, but inside she was really suffering.

This led her to share with me that, if she was being fully honest, it had contributed to her wanting to travel, to escape. She told me that she felt guilty for having been the one who lived, but she also really resented how nobody had thought to ask her if she was okay and how she was coping. She knew they had felt the loss massively too, but now she was older she couldn't stop asking the question how they could have left an eleven-year-old to suffer alone in silence? How could they not have seen the pain she was in?

Now that we understood where her pain had started, we looked for ways we could help her. She really needed to forgive herself so that in time she could forgive her parents for not seeing what she was going through

This brought up so much emotion for her, and I'll admit there were a significant number of tears shed, but the most important piece in all of this was Lisa seeing what she had done to herself. She saw for the first time that she had shut herself off from everything and everyone. She had used travel as an escape tool. Even though she loved it and would never stop doing it, she started to see that there were more things happening all around her in her family and among her friends that required her attention.

She had disconnected but more than that she had lost herself. After almost a year of working together, I could visibly see the changes in Lisa, but when I asked her to sum up what she thought had happened she used these few words: 'I came home to me.'

THOUGHTFUL TOOLS

Complete this Dream Day Exercise below, using all of the detail it conjures up for you to paint the full picture of what your dream day looks like. You're doing this so that you will recognise it when you create it!

Using your own language, describe everything that this day has in it and what you would love to have in it – working on something you love, being in an environment that nourishes you, being surrounded by people who inspire you, or on your own, or indeed both. You can also be in more than one place or one country if that's what you want. Time collapses in your day so include in it whatever you like. The more detail you can put around all of this, the closer you are bringing it towards you. There are no right or wrong answers, only yours.

Include details such as your location, the company you are keeping or if you are flying solo. Describe how you look and what energy you are emitting. Share what you are doing: is it work, rest or play? Portray how you are feeling, and what you're excited for or worried about. Express how you are showing up and presenting yourself and how good that makes you feel.

This might appear like a somewhat pedestrian exercise, but there is power in what it stirs up in each of you. I repeat this exercise myself every few months, and I've never once come up with the same day. You will learn and observe how your needs and desires change and that's a good thing to see!

CHAPTER 9

———————————

PERMISSION TO DETACH FROM THE DRAMA

I KNEW I WAS READY WHEN...

I left every room but never when I should have
I searched everywhere for joy but found none
I ran and hid not quickly but often.
I was angry. I was bitter.
I was ready to fight back. I was ready to attack.
Until I saw that the person I was angry with was me.
The person I was attacking was me.

Niamh Ennis © June 2021

Let's check back in with where you are now and see what you are going to need in order to detach from your drama. So far, you've answered the question *'what matters most to me right now?'*, you've uncovered what your values are and, as a result, you have much greater clarity on what the vision you have for your life looks like. Things are starting to feel a little lighter and a lot more connected. You are preparing yourself for change and transformation.

But before you go full steam ahead, let me ask you, what do you believe has blocked you previously from making changes? What has stopped you from thinking the thought or loving that idea of change, but then in the end always resisting doing anything different? Why do you think that so far you have been unable to release the attachment you've formed between you and your drama?

In order to detach, you must first of all acknowledge that you are indeed attached to your drama and then practice responding in a way that's a lot less dramatic. Possibly without ever being aware you were doing it, your default response has become one of negativity and despair. Your system is now set to see the worst in everything and expect the worst from everyone. It's what feels most familiar to you. Detaching will mean breaking this cycle and opening your heart and mind to greater possibilities.

Would you be prepared to admit that instead of detaching you have found it easier to blame something or someone else for where you find yourself? *'It's not me, it's them!'* The truth is that it will always be easier to apportion blame than to accept it. Accepting it means you have to do something about it and that will require you to leave what feels safest, which right now is your misery and your drama.

When something comes in and turns your life upside down, it leaves you very scared and often quite vulnerable. You are uncertain as to what the real implications of these events are and, equally, you are terrified that it might happen again. This results in you paying far greater attention than normal to your fears, doubts, limiting beliefs and insecurities. That's why you attach yourself to your drama and that's why blaming others comes more naturally to you.

More often than not the act of pointing the finger at others implies that you yourself are not in the best place and may not be feeling at your best. When your confidence is low, it makes it so much more challenging to contemplate doing anything differently.

- How can you possibly put your sights on doing something new when you don't feel you are doing anything right now?
- How can you expect others to back you when you don't even back yourself?
- How can you forgive others when you haven't even yet considered forgiving yourself?
- How can you feel more inspired and motivated to make the changes you so badly want, so you can detach from your drama and begin making rational and transparent decisions again?

You start here by giving yourself permission to change, letting go of the blame, forgiving and learning to first of all love yourself. Cheesy but true.

GRANT YOURSELF PERMISSION

If this sounds simple, it's because it is. Until you give yourself permission to change, nothing changes. You can put all the structures and supports in place, but if you won't allow yourself to do it, what's the point? Permission is normally achieved when you seek and receive approval from another person, but when it comes to living your own life and making decisions about what you want to change, the only person who can possibly give you that permission is you. When you finally give yourself permission to change, change will start happening for you, trust me.

You get so caught up with how things look on the outside that it prevents you from paying proper attention to how they really are on the inside. When you face upheaval in your life, it's normal that you feel sad, upset and disappointed. You do your best to work through the new feelings you experience with varying degrees of success. What you should do is give yourself space to feel how you feel, to let the anger dissipate, the pain fade, and the disappointment fade.

However long it takes is exactly how long it needs to take.

But what you end up doing can look quite different. Somewhere along the way, the reactions of others start to impact you and you find that you deny yourself the chance to start over. You become blind to the signs that you're ready to tentatively step forward again and you get lost in the feeling that you 'must' be seen to behave in a certain way as you navigate your way back.

It is only when you let yourself heal that you can go on and grant yourself permission to detach from the drama in your life. Each ending signals a new beginning. If you can't see that in your life right now, then I ask you to think about all of those times when you felt the world was not on your side? What lessons did you learn, what gifts were hidden in that space, and what good came from a time when you were unable to see anything positive? The answers are there if you just let yourself see them.

When a client comes to me and tells me that they are lost, I hear something different:

- I hear that they have reached their lowest point.
- I hear that they don't want to have to do this on their own.
- And I hear that they are ready to heal.

You need to get to those depths before you are primed to turn and face a different way.

Stop blaming everyone else

I hit on this topic in the previous chapter when I referred to accepting responsibility for your actions, and I truly get that you're hurting, in pain and feeling sad. It's a horrible place to be and I know it can also be a damn lonely one too. But when you get caught in the loop of pain it's all too easy to point the finger elsewhere. *'If only my partner was more attentive'*, *'if only my manager appreciated me more'*, *'if I had a better relationship with my mum'*, *'if I was thinner, richer, more successful'* and on the list goes.

You attach your lack of progress to something external, something outside of you. You separate yourself from all responsibility and you blame other people and other situations for where you are now.

FORGIVE YOURSELF AND OTHERS

What else do you need to do to keep you moving forward? You need to forgive.

I recently decided to forgive someone. Not because they said they were sorry for the hurt they caused me, or because they finally acknowledged the impact the deep pain caused by their actions had had on me, but because I was tired. And I knew that I deserved the peace.

Forgiveness does not mean condoning what someone said or did. That's not a requirement. You don't need to reach a point where you feel okay with what was done or said to you for you to be able to forgive.

Forgiving does not mean that you need to dismiss the truth of how you were hurt. You absolutely don't need to dismiss it; in fact, the more you can acknowledge it, the closer to forgiveness you will get. The more awareness you bring to just how hurt you were and why, the better the chance you have of stopping it from controlling your behaviours.

Forgiveness is about letting go, yes, but it's not about letting anyone off (except unless you count yourself in there). When something happens and you're disappointed or let down, you will experience myriads of emotions. Anything or everything, from rage to anger, betrayal to shock, from pain to sadness.

Forgiveness, as in forgiving yourself and ultimately forgiving others, is the best way to start the process of reconnecting with yourself, as it gives you the permission to detach from the drama, to rewrite your new start and to heal.

What can happen next is that you lose your sense of perspective and simply shut down. You become closed and in some extreme cases you become bitter. This is what separates and disconnects you from all future hope of being able to move on from what happened. You fool yourself into thinking that the best thing you can do for yourself is to put all the necessary barriers in place and that this will stop you from ever getting hurt again (Spoiler: it doesn't!).

By trying to understand what happened, why it happened, what part you played or what part should you have played but didn't, by getting yourself to that next level of understanding, only then can you begin the process of releasing the hold it has on you. Anger, hurt and disappointment control you, but forgiveness releases you.

This is where you really start to give yourself permission to detach slowly from the drama that has been shielding you. Accepting that you can't expect someone else to heal your wounds takes time and strength. Yes, you'll need to lean on others initially as the shock of your hurt or loss sets in. But inevitably you must acknowledge that nobody else is responsible for resolving your own issues but you.

No other person can give you the permission to do that but you. It falls entirely at your feet. Those closest to you can be an integral and necessary part of your healing process. In some cases, they can give you a purpose to carry on, and in others they can provide an incentive to do things better, but you cannot wait for nor expect someone else to come in and do your work. That's down to you!

However, please don't rule out the possibility that other people may in fact be another reason that you are staying attached to your drama. They may not want you to move on as it may suit them and where they are in their lives. They may not want you to grow and thrive, because it will highlight where they are stagnant and stuck. These relationships are best described as 'toxic', simply because they are not good for you and you need to detach from them so that you can in turn detach from your drama.

Letting go of toxicity

Never underestimate how hard it is to let go of people who are intent on making you feel bad about yourself. They could be family members or close friends, but some believe that they can only exist if they keep others down, so watch out for this.

Remember as we referenced earlier that in order for other people to respect you, you need to respect yourself, so start there.

Ask: 'who in my life lifts me up, has my back and celebrates when I sparkle?' These are your people. They give you permission to shine.

Find them. Keep them.

Four indicators that you're surrounded by toxic people

1. It's always all about them. Every conversation is them talking about themselves. They rarely ask questions of you and if they do, you can see that they're waiting for you to stop speaking so they can resume talking about themselves.

2. They rarely celebrate your achievements, even the small ones (especially the small ones). They're unable to be happy for you and often appear resentful.

3. You feel taken advantage of. They use you and you know it. They only ever come looking for you when they need something, or when you have something they need.

4. Despite you stating your needs, they ignore them. They don't respect your boundaries ever and like to appear oblivious to their existence.

Making the decision to move on from people in your life can be really difficult, especially if they don't want to let you go. But there comes a time when you must acknowledge that in order to grow you are going to have to do it without them.

When you choose to make changes in your life, those close

to you may feel a strong resistance to it. Expect that. When you declare that you want better from your life, they hear something different. They hear that you are unhappy with the life they are part of. Your movement unsettles them. It holds a mirror up to their lives, their fears and their insecurities. They are worried as to what this will mean for them and how it will impact them.

Not always knowing why they are doing this, they'll try to talk you out of it. They might not always want you to be unhappy, but what they are really saying is that they don't want you to be happier *without* them. They are doing what feels natural and looking after their own best interests. Simply put, you need to do the same.

Some toxic people will go a step further and aim to reinforce your own doubts and limiting beliefs. When you think '*I can't do this*', they'll be there ready to agree that you can't and you shouldn't. When you think '*what it will look like to others, will they think I'm getting notions above my station?*', they'll point to failure, judgement and criticism when what you really need to hear is encouragement and support.

They can only do this if you let them. So don't let them. Extricate yourself from their company. Find the people who want what's best for you, who want to see you grow and who will cheer you on from the sides and be there when you cross the line.

Respond don't react

As you detach from the drama, I'd invite you to be aware of how you respond rather than react. When you react, you default to your old way of doing things, which may not always be the right way. You engage your emotions and act out how you feel about something in that moment. When you respond, you are more likely to think of the real impact of your actions and are far more likely to present them in a rational and coherent way. Your instant reactions tend to be solely emotional, so watch out to ensure both are present – the emotional and the rational.

Be unapologetically you

Not everyone will understand why your desires mean so much to you or even why it is that you feel a need to change. Some will likely feel threatened by your desire to expand and grow, but that's okay. Not everyone needs to understand why you want this so much. It's up to you to connect to your 'why' – why you want this, why it matters so much to you and how you want to feel when you have it.

Never apologise to anyone for wanting to be more than you are right now

Instead, grant yourself permission and offer an apology to yourself for having waited this long to do anything about it. You spend the first part of your life trying to fit in, to simply be the same as everyone else, not wanting to stand out, and then you reach this later stage where you ask, *'why do I really need to keep doing that?'* Why indeed!

Don't become what happened to you, become who you are because of it

Your magic is you. One thing that you have that nobody else has is you. Your voice, your story, your soul, your mind and your values. If you are doing all of this for the right reason, if you are doing this entirely for yourself, then nobody needs an explanation. You will do it, and let me tell you, you'll do it very well if it comes from that honest place in your heart that makes it feel real. The other thing that you also have that nobody else has either is your life. This one precious life. Live it like you love it. And you soon will.

Life-changing events do just that, they change your life. They alter how you view the world, how you show up and how you want to be seen. What mattered before rarely matters again. And that's okay. It's also perfectly okay for you to feel that you are done feeling low and feeling sad. You're allowed to feel tired of being so angry with the world all of the time. You're allowed to feel exhausted being the one that people feel sorry for. You are allowed to feel however it is you feel.

You crave a return to who you were before this life-changing event happened, but you also know that it's simply not possible. You cannot be her again because you have changed, but you can be better than who you are now. Much better.

So, promise me and yourself that you will keep pointing in the right direction, you will keep striving to feel better and to be better. And that you will do this all unapologetically.

There is beauty in simplicity

It's finally time to let go. To release, to detach, to move on with your life; not away from it but on with it. There's no right or wrong way to approach this. You start only when you feel ready to start. The magic in you gets to choose not only how you live your life but also how you view it and how you feel in it. I believe that the most beautiful lives become the simplest ones. By simple, I don't mean you have to put all your earthly goods on e-Bay and go live on a mountain in the Himalayas, I mean stripping everything right back until you are left with nothing except the people and things that matter most to you.

You recognise that when things are good you're better able to keep moving ahead. And when things are not so good, you need to pause, feel, heal and then reset your compass and take the time to decide where to go next. The simplicity is in that pause. It's in that moment when you go inwards and watch for the shoots of joy. They may not be plentiful, they may be sparse, but they are there and when you notice them, I promise you, more will appear.

There is such beauty in simplicity. I know it is no coincidence that these past few years have been the richest, most rewarding and meaningful of my life while also being the simplest. My days are filled with walking in the woods, touching trees, writing, being of service in my work and, for sheer balance, watching reality television in the company of my dog. I've never been happier. There's a stillness here in me that I could only have gotten from my dad guiding me to this place at this time in my life.

I honestly don't think I will be here always, as Dublin has never really left my heart, but I will always feel deeply grateful to Galway for healing me. I have no idea where the future will take me but, incredibly, I don't need to. I know I am being minded.

When you feel stronger, you'll feel ready to let your courage speak to you. Listen and let yourself be led by it. It will take you to beautiful places. Listen for the whispers, listen to the nudges from your internal guide, your soul. Listen to the sounds that surround you. Surrender to them. When you can't see, always listen. When you surrender to the beauty around you, nothing ends. Everything begins.

THOUGHTFUL TOOLS

If that person who hurt you is no longer around and you find that you are left with a lot of unresolved issues with no opportunity to speak your mind, why not choose to write to them? In your letter, express exactly how you are feeling. Say everything that you've wanted to say for so long but never had the chance. Write until you've nothing left to write. Then go outside in the night air and burn that letter. The energy you carried with you has left you and has now gone up in flames and you will feel all the lighter for it. This is a very simple but extremely powerful way of letting go of any buried thoughts and feelings.

Consider where you need forgiveness in your own life right now? Think about who it is you need to forgive so that you can feel free again. By discovering what anger and resentments you are holding onto, you'll see what is in fact holding *you* back.

A REMEMBERING

If you don't give yourself permission to feel the pain, you cannot heal the pain.

If you don't allow yourself to sit with the anger, you won't be free from it.

If you don't give yourself permission to cry with the sadness, you won't escape it.

You must feel it all to heal it all.

CHAPTER 10

REWRITE YOUR STORY

In Chapter 2, we investigated your old stories and I invited you to observe and explore what these were and where they might have come from. I'm going to assume now, that by identifying them, you have a good idea of the ones you want to change and the ones that might need to be rewritten.

You might already recognise a pattern or story around you that has been dimming your light, just so that you could avoid being noticed, and it has enabled you to stay where you felt it was safe because it was familiar. But you also know now that you're less likely to push yourself to grow, to change and to expand when you remain stuck in that safe place.

If this feels right for you, if this feels like you, then you are ready to rewrite your story.

Think of your life like that page-turner you enjoy reading. You're so invested in the main character. You want nothing but the best outcome for her. You're willing her on the entire time.

You're nervous when she faces challenges and so incredibly proud of her when she overcomes them. But this is you now. This is your story and your life. It's no longer just a character on a page.

You get to create what happens next for her and for you. You design who it is she relates to, what she does, where she goes and how she shows up. She is you. You get to craft each chapter, set the theme ahead of time, select how the plot unfolds (which other characters will feature in) and you decide how it will all come together and feel. That's what real power feels like and it's entirely within your reach.

When you think of the stories that have influenced you, you think about and are inspired by the lives of your mothers, sisters or friends. I want you to think of those who have gone before you in your families as women, just like you. Think of the obstacles they faced, the struggles they encountered and the joy they created from having so much less. In committing to your own healing, you are healing all of those who have gone before you. Don't ever forget that.

Who are you, really?

I want that, when you think of your story, you see yourself as the main character. Not by what you do, but by who you are. Describe her in detail. Perhaps start with how you would ideally like her to be and use this to prompt you into connecting with where you are now. This will show you the short distance between your present and your future. Be warned that you might not like what you identify in yourself today, but that's the beauty of all of this. Awareness heals and by seeing those parts of you that you would like to change and accepting that this change is your choice, you are now connecting with the woman you are becoming. The way forward is already presenting itself to you.

What is it you want?

Tune back into the work you've done already on creating your vision and simply add in as much detail and colour here to include:

- What qualities will your main character, *you*, need to have to make this story real?
- How will she feel when she is living out her new story?
- How will she show up in each chapter?
- Will she witness growth and expansion?
- What steps can you take right now to bring this story to life?

Please, please make sure that the detail you are arriving at is yours and yours alone. Resist the urge to think about the life you *should* create or the story you are *expected* to write; think only of the one you want. Suspend what you know those close to you would want to see you do and focus entirely on yourself. If what you uncover is your truth and your authentic desires, if it comes directly from your heart-space and not your head, then the Universe will hear your call and will reply appropriately.

Of that, I am absolutely sure.

CLIENT CONVERSATIONS – SAMMY

Sammy came to work with me having decided to set up a new online business. She was deeply unhappy in her senior role in IT and had spent the last year dreaming of doing something that felt more purposeful.

Her biggest concern was that she wouldn't be taken seriously. This was borne out by the fact that those closest to her – her mum, her partner and even her manager – had all used the word 'flighty' when describing her. She preferred to view it as proof that she was on a constant quest towards fulfilling her dream!

When we explored this notion and attempted to get greater clarity for her on just what that dream would look like, I noticed some discrepancies appearing. She described herself as restless and unsettled, but what I started to observe was someone who was simply scared of being in the same place for too long. She talked about how there had to be something more out there for her, that she was desperate to live a life she could feel proud of with no regrets. Yet, what was proving increasingly impossible to ignore was that her words weren't matching her actions.

I pushed her to explore why she felt she was always in such a hurry to prove herself, why she thought she had never reached a place in her life that felt right for her and what sitting still would look and feel like for a while. I challenged her to consider what would happen if she accepted that where she was in her life right now was where she was supposed to be, and that perhaps she needed to sit still and be for while?

Apart from the look of sheer horror etched all over her face, she couldn't but let out a physical gasp. The idea of this was simply abhorrent to her. 'Sitting still is so new-agey', were the first words out of her mouth. 'I honestly can't tolerate all this indulgence I see for finding or connecting with yourself. I just want an action plan and let me at it! Isn't that what you do, Niamh?' Yes, yes, it is but it isn't what I was going to do here. Well, not to start with!

I needed Sammy to understand where this restlessness had originated and what was it telling her. Together, we were beginning to build a foundation of deep trust and in our next session she referred to her dad. 'Some girls have these beautiful stories of dads and their daughters. I don't. I have none. My dad left my mum when I was five. I've two older sisters who were eight and twelve. My mum had thrown him out. I was never quite sure of the full details, only that they had rowed a lot and our house was drowning in that tension. One day he was there the next he wasn't. I didn't know enough about what happened to understand that it wasn't my fault. Nobody reassured me either that it wasn't, so for quite a while I believed that something I did, or didn't do, had contributed to him leaving.

'I grew up fiercely independent as a result. I didn't want anyone to think I needed anything from them, I wanted them to see I was good on my own and self-sufficient. If I didn't depend on them, they wouldn't feel that pressure and they wouldn't leave. They wouldn't do what Dad had done.

'As I got older and could understand more, Mum explained that our dad had actually had a gambling problem and quite a serious one. He'd lost all their savings along with his job and had secretly re-mortgaged the house. It sounded a little like something from a movie, but it left Mum and the three of us in quite a pickle! Mum's parents offered to help her out but only if she asked him to leave. I can see now how incredibly difficult this was for her. She did what she did for us and yet I had harboured so much resentment towards her for years.

'How I felt towards both him and her had reinforced my

story that you can't ever depend on anyone or trust them. You need to keep moving. Keep looking out for the next job, the next career, the next friend and even the next partner. I was always preparing for something to go wrong. When you think like this, it usually does.'

Sammy has a lovely connection with her mum now, but this story of not being able to depend on anyone for anything had and still does really impact her life. It's why she jumps from one relationship to another and is so incredibly scared of commitment. It's why she is obsessed with saving money for the rainy day and it is definitely why she moves from one company to the next in search of something better.

Her story, the one she created to protect herself as a child, is still very present today. If she keeps moving, relies on nobody, is financially independent and shows up as a strong powerful woman, she will remain untouchable.

We had quite a bit of work to do. This traumatic event in Sammy's life had become lodged in her brain and that sense of abandonment that she had experienced but never articulated resulted in her leaning into a story of 'I can do this all on my own!' We worked together on making her aware of how her money story was also dictating how she lived her life, how every decision she made was coming from that place of fear and lack.

We started to rewrite her story. I helped her become aware that the current one she was attached to was not even hers; it belonged to her mum but had been absorbed by her. With no judgement at all, I needed her to see that she had the power and ability to create her own story now. A new one that would serve the person she was becoming, rather than being stuck in the past.

I also wanted her to witness the gift of being able to reach out and ask for help. We tackled her fears of doing this head-on until we slowly started to unpack them. I watched as she slowly realised that being able to express her vulnerability was the best way to rebuild connection and see it for the act of strength that it is.

It truly was such a beautiful experience watching her unfold in front of me and it still is the only time I have sat with a client while we both openly cried at her transformation, but watching her bloom and grow, witnessing her release her need to control so much and seeing her detach from her old story so that she could rewrite a fresh new one reminded me why doing this work is so incredible.

Where to begin rewriting your story

To help you begin, I'm sharing my own experience of what the rewriting of my own story looked like for me. I had subconsciously created stories around myself that were not only untrue but very limiting. They were blocking me from moving forward, stopping me from doing anything new or different. I felt safe hiding behind these stories, so I didn't question them. They just were.

My story went something like this…

I believed I was the girl who bad things happened to. I believed I was liked but not really loved. I felt I was enjoyed but rarely missed. I was ambitious but never the best. I believed I was, in all parts of my life, a silver medallist. My mother prepared me well for this role. She encouraged me to be comfortable with being a great number two. She said I was a super support act. She made me feel like I was born for it and I felt this as a small child. It continued well into my teenage years. Never holding gold, never achieving first place.

I was always almost there but never quite at the front. I never won at anything but came second and was joint-winner a lot. I was never someone's first choice, but I was constantly their second. I even got a second-class honours degree from university. I got offered so many great jobs, but only after someone else declined. It wasn't the worst place to be, but I had no concept of what being in the best place – the first place – would feel like. I had only known second place because I'd been told to expect it.

This story was said to me with love. I do believe that. It was said to me to protect me from feeling let down, but in fact what it started was a lifetime of preparing for disappointment, as I believed this was my reality while it didn't have to be. The truth is that this was someone else's story and not mine. Yet it became mine. My response was to try and control it, to pre-empt all the worst-case scenarios, to put in place all the structures I knew of that would protect me.

This resulted in me living my life from a place of fear. Thinking that everything around me was constantly changing and trying to control my life rather than just living my life resulted in me missing out on so much.

The story I wanted to live

I'd spent so long living in this story that I didn't feel worthy or deserving of being more or of doing what it was I really wanted. Whenever I thought of my dream life it had always involved writing, but I would remind myself that to be a writer you had to be the best writer, and I would stop myself right there from doing anything more about it. What I actually needed to do was devise a narrative that would allow me to understand that I didn't need to be the best as long as I was doing what I loved. If I was listening to my heart, to what it wanted, I would do what I loved and what I wanted.

Thankfully, I have done this and I choose now to think about it differently. It no longer matters to me whether I am first, second or even third. I'm no longer blaming my mother or equating success with coming first. I trust that this life I am living, and me doing what I am doing, is the right one for me. What matters most is that I feel safe to be the full version of myself.

This also marked the beginning of my personal reconnection, because it was only at this point that I felt ready and gave myself permission to take charge and rewrite my own story. By tuning in to what I wanted and how I wanted to feel, I was also learning how to block out other people's opinions and judgements. I was declaring that the main character was going to be very different from who I was now and she certainly didn't need a medal to prove it.

When you are doing this, I call on you to begin from a place of confidence and self-belief. You alone have the power to shape your own future. By releasing the stories and judgements that others place on you, you get to start with your very own blank page.

As you rewrite your story, I invite you to consider the following:

- Who you are now and who you are becoming?
- Who is this magical woman at the heart of your story, how does she feel and what does she need?
- Ask her what lights her up, what makes her feel free and safe, and does she believe she can love and be loved?

Discover what needs to happen for her to feel free to be the full version of herself. You need to ask because she needs the opportunity to tell you! These answers will tell you all you need to know about yourself; the rest is just dressing and noise.

What can you do to change this now?

Begin by breaking your story down into more digestible parts. Who is it you want to become? Be clear on what the full version of your life looks like. Don't rush to the end. Think about what it is you would like to do next and where you want to end. Divide your life up into your relationships, spirituality, friendships, career, health, learning and creativity and consider what parts need a total rewrite and in what order? Where will your focus go? You may come across sections or people that need to be edited out. Let them go.

Be ruthless in being kind to yourself. Give yourself plenty of space to observe where you are tolerating behaviour from others that is not acceptable. Resolve to build better boundaries and promise yourself that this time you will stick to them. Show yourself the love that you've been missing from your life on each and every page of your new story.

You've earned this

The reason you stayed where you were and didn't make attempts to bring about the transformation you wanted was perhaps because you didn't believe you deserved a life any better than the one you were in. You convinced yourself or allowed yourself be convinced by the idea that you should be grateful for what you had, and so you settled where you found yourself. You felt guilty for asking for more. You told yourself others had it worse, and those that have it better were clearly more deserving of it.

You can subscribe to any version of this that you need to; or you can allow yourself to believe that you do deserve to be happy, to be abundant and successful just as much as anyone else does. Because you do. Have you considered that those who appear happier, more successful and more abundant trust that they fundamentally deserve to have what they have? The question is then, why don't you feel the same?

I want you to document your declaration that you are giving yourself permission to receive what you deserve. I want you to write that into your story and create affirmations that will remind you on a daily basis. To help, here are some affirmations that I use:

- It is safe for me to be the full version of myself.
- I love the woman I am becoming. She excites me.
- I deserve and expect the best. It's who I am now.
- I am committed to my goals and that's why I am unstoppable.
- My success is inevitable.
- I surrender to the magic of my life and all that it has to offer.
- I have the courage to keep going.
- I welcome in all that serves me and is for my highest good.
- I love this life, my life and the life I am creating.
- The best is yet to come, yet everything is perfect now.
- I have what it takes to manifest the life of my dreams.
- I listen to the whispers of my soul and trust what it tells me always.
- Everything is always working out for me.

I invite you now to reclaim your power in a much more confident manner. We will explore ways to restore your confidence in the next chapter, but for now I want you to realise that what's happening is you are calling your power back in. Listen to that part of you that knows what you want. The part that has always known, that has always tried to guide you home when you were only ever interested in going in the opposite direction.

Think of rewriting the story of your life as removing all the complicated sub-themes; deleting the plot twists that only feature for dramatic effect; replacing all the toxic characters that are only there to add colour. Replace them with what and who makes you feel good. Who makes you laugh, who makes you feel loved and who makes you feel good about yourself when you are in their company? Then insert them into more of your chapters.

What happened to me is not who I am. I get to decide who I am becoming now.

When you start to step into your true power and wrap yourself up in the rewriting of your story, you're also sending out a powerful message and letting the world see that you believe change and transformation are not just possible, but that they are entirely possible for you. You're choosing to do things differently because you want to feel differently. You want to feel connected again.

The measure of your ability to live a full life is not based on having had an easy life, but being determined to make it the happiest one you can. Think of the power that exists in that feeling and just how strong it makes you feel inside.

It's time to start creating your new story. In doing so, I hope you find the courage, the bravery and optimism to transform your life. I want you to have not simply rewritten your story, but to have lived it fully and enthusiastically with no regrets, right to the last chapter, to the epilogue.

I hope for you that you can feel the tiredness that only exhausting yourself doing what you love brings. That you know when to pause between chapters, when to inhale, when to reflect and when you need to take your pen back out and make some fresh edits. I hope you are never afraid again to make fresh edits.

THOUGHTFUL TOOLS

• Who inspires you to be better, to do better?

• Who is the woman you want to become?

To help you get started on creating your own Daily Affirmations I have created this <u>PDF</u> document for you. http://www.niamhennis.com/affirmations

A REMEMBERING

Stop denying your own story. Feel proud of it all. You are who you are and it defines you. When you take full ownership over it and accept responsibility for exactly how it unfolds, you are declaring yourself ready to complete your beautiful and honest ending.

CHAPTER 11

RESTORE YOUR CONFIDENCE

Self-worth, self-belief and confidence are all ways of describing the act of loving yourself more. It's about backing yourself and captaining your own team, leading yourself out on the pitch. It means giving yourself the exact same respect, compassion and understanding you so easily give to others. Your mind believes everything that you tell it. So why not tell yourself a better story? It doesn't even have to be true; you only have to believe it!

When you were a child, you didn't consider before shining brightly. You just shone. You were born and entered the world in a luminous state. You didn't know yet what it was to worry about the small stuff, to doubt people and to judge people. You only knew love. But you didn't even know properly that's what it was yet. As you move through life, that changes. You react to the behaviour of others; you respond to the absence of love and nourishment, and you slowly learn how to protect

167

yourself so that you give yourself the best chance of survival.

As you carry on living, events and experiences arise that can cause you to question your own self-belief; you're told to dim your light, so you shrink to fit in. Your voice gets quieter and your self-confidence slowly fades. You simply cannot pretend that your self-confidence and self-assurance is unaffected by the opinions of others. It is. Sometimes, without even needing to speak to them, you make the assumption that you already know exactly what they are thinking, and what's worse is that you go on to make decisions from this place.

Think of Florrie in your accounts department at work. She sits happily, every day, gossiping about everyone and everything. We all know a Florrie. You know she does this. Heavens, she's done it often enough both with you and in front of you. You're scared that one day it will be you she's talking about, and it will! But Florrie, and all the Florrie's in the world, carry quite a lot of influence over what you do and how you behave without you even being aware of it. You silently and easily hand your power over into their hands.

You think of them when you are about to make decisions, you wonder what they will say when word gets around that you are leaving your relationship, signing up for a health programme, launching a new business, producing pieces of art, letting your singing voice be heard in public for the first time, or writing the book you always promised yourself you would. You remember Florrie and you stop. You shrink.

The truth is that there will always be people who remark on what you are doing. You can continue to pay attention to them or you can choose to end it by deciding what success looks like for you. What do you need that will make you feel proud of who you are and what you are doing so you can make all your decisions from there?

To hell with the Florrie's of this world. You know they're going to talk one way or another, but don't let them talk you out of chasing your dreams. When you get to the end of your days, do you think there's even the slightest chance that you might say to yourself *'I'm glad I didn't do that, and I didn't give them the chance to judge me?'* Er, no, you won't! I can absolutely guarantee you that you won't even know their names, let alone what their opinions might be!

Next time you find yourself doing this, ask yourself, does Florrie's opinion really matter to me? I think we all know the answer to that one!

Can I also ask, why are you so quick to hand your power over to someone else? Why do you believe that your life is somehow less valuable, less important than everyone else's? I'm interested to know where this belief started for you and when it was that you chose to become someone else.

These questions may appear intrusive (and they are) but the impact these answers have on your life is very real, and have themselves had a dramatic influence on how you show up in the world. Along the way, someone told you that you were too much or not enough. Along the way, you listened to and believed them. You gave them the power to take back your confidence and belief in yourself. You handed it back to them. You did this. Nobody else. You.

So, if you gave it, you can take it back. You can change it by understanding where and when it happened. By identifying exactly who was there when it happened, you can bring a new awareness that will release you from it. Now that you know when it was taken from you, you also get to decide when it returns.

Everything you dream of being, you once were. Read that again if you need to. Everything you dream of being, you once were. It's now time to resurrect this part of you once again.

- The ability to believe in yourself so strongly that the opinions of others don't influence you anymore.
- The confidence to know that with some determination and assistance you can achieve what you need to.
- The belief that asking for help will fast-track you to where you want to get to.
- The knowledge that change is not just for other people and that their successes don't and won't ever in any way detract from yours.

THE BENEFIT OF HINDSIGHT

When you begin to understand why you are here and what your purpose is, it encourages you to be more confident with who it is you truly are and what unique gifts you can bring into this world. It permits you to celebrate your differences rather than hide them.

Six-year-old Niamh felt called to write, but twenty-five-year-old Niamh told her quite firmly that it wasn't a financially viable career. Forty-year-old Niamh looked with envy at all of those who were doing what they loved and really felt that she had missed her chance. Fifty-year-old Niamh finally conceded that writing made her happy. She didn't need to be any good at it, she didn't even need others to tell her that she was any good at it, she just needed to exercise that part of her that believed all along that her purpose was to write. This book is the evidence.

I witness my clients doing the same thing. I create space for them to see and hear what their soul is asking of them. When you agree to listen to the whispers, the message is unmistakable. This can happen for you too when you allow for this space to appear. Don't try to silence your heart's desire. If you talk all the time about listening to what your soul is telling you that your heart wants, then you also need to find the courage to act on it. Ideas without actions are unfulfilled promises, so make a realistic plan and do what needs to be done.

DO YOU FEEL SAFE TO BE YOU?

I know that some of this might still feel a little bit too aspirational. When I was at my lowest, nothing triggered me more than someone telling me I needed to feel more confident. You too might be feeling somewhat overwhelmed and worried that your days of feeling confident are well behind you, but I believe that all feelings of confidence are rooted in that place where you feel most safe to be the full version of yourself. So where is that for you?

Put another way, do you feel safe to be you where you are now? Do you feel able amongst your friends, family and colleagues to be as you are? Do you feel free to express your own personal thoughts, opinions and feelings?

I'm not asking you to revisit your people-pleasing tendencies. I'm talking about that feeling inside where you are able to be your most real, authentic and true self. If you don't currently feel safe, then this may require some more in-depth examination of your relationships and friendships.

- Can you think of a time when you left a gathering of your friends feeling deflated, perhaps because you felt you weren't being included?
- At work, do you feel encouraged to contribute openly

to discussions?

- Within your family, do you feel that they value your opinions or that your partner listens to what it is you need from them?

These answers will help you see not only where you are not being heard but how much it impacts you. You now know that when you feel safe to express your thoughts, opinions or feelings you feel valued, and when you feel valued you feel heard. You also now know that when you feel others are listening, you feel better in yourself and about yourself. That's why this matters so much.

THOUGHTFUL TOOLS

To feel safe

- What would it really feel like if you felt safe?
- When did you last feel safe and who was there?
- What/who makes you feel unsafe?
- What two things can you do this week to move you closer to feeling safe?

How you show up in the world

- Select eight words those who know you best would use to describe you.
- Select eight words that you believe best describe you as you are today.
- Select eight more that best describe how you would love to be seen.

CHAPTER 12

BUILD BETTER BOUNDARIES

Whenever I raise the subject of boundaries with my clients, I tend to be met with instant resistance to the concept that is purely based on a misguided belief that boundaries are negative, selfish and wrong. But I get this. I think the word 'boundary' itself conjures up images of a physical separation or something that divides us, which couldn't be further from the truth. Good, healthy boundaries can in fact pull you much closer to the people you love.

It is my personal belief that a boundary is a personal limit within which you can openly communicate how it is that you expect to be treated. It is something you commit to achieving, regardless of whether it is offered or given. It is never about you apportioning blame to others for how they act; it is about you taking responsibility to change what poor behaviour you accept and tolerate from others.

Never have you needed boundaries more than in today's

world. Living through the recent pandemic reinforced for many of you that you each have a responsibility to look after yourself so that you can in turn be ready to show up for others. Which is in fact what boundaries also do: they serve to protect you. The individual protecting themselves is the very best way for you to contribute towards the benefit of the collective.

Boundaries receive so much negative press simply because you are afraid that, if you attempt to put them in place, people will think you are being selfish, or that you might offend those you love. You worry also that you might stop being needed if you were to implement them, but equally, you are also nervous that you might not be able to sustain them, which will result in you giving in, again.

Boundaries are not about you changing someone else's behaviour – they are about you changing how you react to their actions. This is why you are afraid to want them or implement them. Often, you don't even know what specifically it is that you need, you just know that you can't keep putting other people's needs so far ahead of your own. But you are also not always clear where to even start with prioritising yourself in a way that feels comfortable. All of that is natural and common.

How do you know when you need better boundaries?

1. You feel resentment rising inside of you.

2. You know that people are taking advantage of you.

3. You hear yourself repeatedly complaining that others are crossing your boundaries.

4. You feel nobody ever takes your needs into account and yet you're expected to be available for others all the time.

5. You're overlooked and are under-appreciated at work.

6. You tolerate behaviour from others that you absolutely know to be disrespectful.

We've discussed in previous chapters just how empowering it will be when you reclaim those parts of your lives that connect you, when you learn to do what matters most to you with who matters most. Setting boundaries is the starting point for this work. Without them, your foundations for dreaming of doing things differently will forever remain unsteady.

Boundaries are about protecting your energy also

Try to remember that boundaries are not something that should make you miserable. If you are nervous about putting boundaries in place it is mostly because you're afraid of how they will be received and that they will make you less likeable. The reverse tends in fact to be true. If you set better boundaries, you will then attract those who are willing to respect your decisions and want nothing but the best for you. Honestly, how great does that sound?

CLIENT CONVERSATIONS – CHLOE

When Chloe first came to see me, she talked about feeling like she was invisible and that nobody really appreciated or attempted to understand what was happening to her or how she was feeling now. This included her family and close friends. She was also quick to point out that she knew they'd be shocked and stunned if they heard her saying this. Her exact words were, 'of course they think I'm doing well, because they never, ever ask'.

I was struck by the level of bitterness and sadness in her voice. She sounded so deeply frustrated and described a situation where she felt like she was the one that everyone called on morning, noon and night. They had helped her once and she now felt like she was going to spend the rest of her life repaying them!

When I raised the subject of putting boundaries in place, it was most interesting. Listening to her talk about friends in her circle who she recognised as having quite good boundaries was also very telling. She described this aspect of them as extremely self-serving and selfish. Yet, she also admitted to being insanely envious of their ability to say 'no' to others and do what they wanted. I remember her asking me, 'how do they know what they want? I've no idea what I want from life, none!' This was exactly the place we started on when beginning our work together on Chloe's boundaries.

What Chloe identified in these first thoughts about boundaries is exactly what so many of us experience – that innate contradiction, of wanting more for ourselves of what we criticise in others. Chloe felt invisible, she didn't feel heard, she felt taken for granted and overlooked; and underneath it all, she knew that she was partly to blame for this herself.

Chloe had been a very young widower. Her husband Charlie

had died in a car crash eleven years ago. They hadn't had any children together when he died, so Chloe had been very reliant on her mother and sisters to get her through those early years. More recently though, she was really feeling like they were calling back in the favours. Not a day went by when she wouldn't get a phone call from some family member asking her to run an errand, or looking for her to listen to their latest grumble. If she dared say that she was busy or wasn't available, she would be quickly met with a 'sure, what else are you doing?'

Chloe's family had become so used to her being there that in truth they actually believed they were doing a favour by including her in every single detail of their lives. They were oblivious that she needed her own space or that she in fact craved it. Their intention was pure, it came from a place of love, and in their minds, they were still trying to help Chloe by keeping her busy. They had no idea that their actions were having the opposite effect and were in fact holding her back. Chloe and I spoke about what she wanted from all of this. She knew something was going to have to change, but she was beyond scared to do anything.

So, we began by helping her get clarity on what the desired outcome was for her. If she wasn't afraid and felt free to express her needs, what would they be?

'I want space. I want to feel that I can live my own life and not have my every single move scrutinised. I want to be free to make my own choices about what I do, where I go and who I spend my time with. I love and appreciate them but they are suffocating me and I just don't know how to tell them that without causing offence or having them start to worry about me again.'

Chloe felt cornered. She felt that if she spoke up they would be insulted and yet if she didn't, she'd go mad! What was needed was an opportunity for her to have a conversation first with the sister she felt closest to.

She needed to communicate that while she appreciated how much they had done for her and would never forget it, she desperately needed some space now for her to see what she could do to regain her own independence. She knew this might upset them, as it would imply she would be less available while uncovering what it was in her life that she wanted to do and focusing on herself a little more.

So, she began by talking to the sister she felt would understand this the most. She explained how she honestly felt and asked her sister for help when it came to sharing this with the rest of the family. When she did choose to speak to the wider family, she used positive language and avoided all accusatory statements. She worried they would listen but not hear, so she framed it in such a way that they would clearly understand this wasn't just what she wanted but what needed to happen.

Admittedly, a few further follow-up conversations had to happen, as some of her family members struggled with this concept more than others, and on quite a few occasions it required her having to be a little more forthright in saying 'no'. But eventually, they all got there.

In setting boundaries, Chloe saw the importance of getting clarity on what she really wanted. But equally important was staying consistent with these boundaries and not going back on what it was she had asked for. She now loves the time she spends with her family and they are in fact much happier seeing her so content in herself.

Boundaries help you connect to yourself more deeply, to that intuitive part where healing happens. They provide you with a solid basis for all your future relationships, starting of course with the most important one of all: the one we have with ourselves.

If you are disconnected and repeatedly putting others' needs ahead of your own, then you simply don't know what it is that you want. If you don't know what you want, you most definitely don't know how to ask for it and so the cycle continues.

THREE STAGES TO BUILDING BETTER BOUNDARIES.

STAGE ONE – NAME IT SO YOU CAN TAME IT

The first step when it comes to boundary-setting is knowing what you want and getting real clarity on that. To help, have a think about what currently triggers you. What behaviour do you find unacceptable and intolerable, and if you find one, think about who is responsible for it? Then really explore what is it that you need to do to ensure your needs are being met.

When you stop and think, ask yourself honestly what is it that you could do more of if you had the time? You deserve this and more. An important reminder, as you're doing this, that boundaries are never for other people, they are for you.

They should protect you, support you and remind you of your own self-worth. By naming just what it is that is causing you to demand better boundaries for yourself, you are now starting to connect to that inner voice, which is suggesting to you what's more acceptable to you and what will make you feel happier once you implement it. Then you can tame it.

Examine the people and events in your life. Look at your diary for the next month. When you see the appointments scheduled in, how does each one make you feel? Are you excited and looking forward to that lunch or dinner, or are you filled with dread at the mere prospect? There's a lot of information to be found in your answer!

Think about events or engagements you attended in the past month. How were you left feeling in the aftermath of each of them? Depleted or nourished? *Please, as always, be honest with your answers.* Notice the patterns that emerge either in the offenders or your reaction. What you're searching for here is the information that will lead you towards feeling safer, more loved and more valued.

STAGE TWO - IF YOU'RE EXPLAINING, YOU'RE LOSING

Now that you know which boundaries you're going to start with, your next step is to decide just how you are going to communicate those boundaries. But, and this is crucial, I want you to note that not every boundary needs to be shared, even with the person you're setting the boundary with! The reason for this is that the boundary is not for anyone else but you, so have a think about how you can effectively achieve it and what you will benefit from telling them, and whether you truly believe that it needs to be shared.

If it merely requires you to pull back, to start saying 'no' more often and be less available, then don't feel that you always need to communicate what you're doing. Sometimes, I find this can be quite a deterrent in getting started – the fear we experience about what to say and how it will be received – so really think about what will work best for you given the boundary you are addressing and the person you are protecting yourself from.

There are, of course, other situations where communication

is an integral and vital part of the process. When we communicate our boundaries in a clear and succinct way, we are setting our intentions very clearly and paving the way for great changes.

MIND YOUR LANGUAGE

I can't overstate the importance of carefully choosing the language you use when the time comes to communicate and express your boundaries. No matter how tempted you might feel to stray into emotional territory, please don't. Just stick with the absolute facts. Always speak with confidence, but be respectful and never confrontational. Do not let this decline into being argumentative or accusatory. Avoid using phrases such as *'you always say/do this'* or *'it really irritates me when you say this...'* or *'Why do you keep doing this?'* Phrases like these can feel very aggressive if you are on the receiving end, and if someone feels attacked they'll do what feels natural and simply defend themselves.

Consider the timing. The best place to have these conversations is on neutral ground at a time when both parties are feeling a little more relaxed. Please also remember that the person you're speaking to will have had zero time to prepare a thoughtful response. You'll most likely have caught them off-guard, so don't react to their first response. Ideally, you want to say to them at the start that you're not expecting a response, that you are aware this might not be what they were expecting to hear, and that if they wish you could schedule another coming together at a mutually convenient time. This will afford them a chance to offer a reply that will more accurately reflect their true feelings.

This is not about blame or pointing the finger. This is about you wishing to build a better boundary to protect yourself, and once again it is not about you changing their behaviour, but changing how you let it impact you.

Finally, in case you need to hear this, here's a little reminder that you are not doing anything wrong. Wanting to protect yourself is never selfish. And trust me, the feeling you get when you put boundaries in place will be in itself such a powerful reward on so many levels that you'll wonder why it took you so long to do it!

When you reach the end of this chapter, you'll have one question: *'how will I know if I have successfully implemented a boundary?'* Spoiler alert: you'll feel so incredibly guilty!

You'll feel tormented by guilt and will be tempted to rush back and say *'forget I said anything!'* Ignore this feeling, at all costs! Resentment is an indicator that you needed better boundaries and guilt is the sign that you are implementing them. Just prepare yourself to feel this way.

YOUR 'GETTING STARTED WITH BOUNDARIES' TEMPLATE

Using an example of a sister called Eva who is prone to making inappropriate comments towards another sister when the family is gathered, let's look at what to say and how to navigate that awkward conversation:

'Eva, I have decided that I need to be clearer on how I'd like those close to me to treat me. I hope you'll appreciate how important this is to me and just what it means for me to have this conversation with you. You're my sister, Eva, and I love and respect you. You know this. But when you make comments and jokes about my weight in front of the entire family, I feel utterly

crushed and disrespected. I'd like to ask that you stop commenting on my appearance. If this continues, Eva, I will excuse myself from all future family occasions that you are attending.'

Clearly, what we are addressing here is not a one-off throwaway remark by Eva, but a repeatedly persistent and disrespectful taking down of her sister, most likely to make herself feel better. No matter what the reasons or whether she was aware she was doing it, a boundary has now been set. Feel free to substitute Eva for your manager, partner, friend or work colleague and think about what you will do if the request is denied. Always stay calm during your delivery; don't get swept up in the emotion of it all. Be the swan appearing graceful on top, despite what you're feeling underneath! Consider that their first response may be a defensive one and be conscious of the language you are using. It might also seem a little obvious, but invest time to practice in advance what you're going to say. If it helps, stand in front of the mirror rehearsing until it becomes what you end up saying.

Possible responses when you struggle with saying 'no' and are keen to set boundaries:

If someone invites you to something that you don't want to go to simply say:

'That sounds like a fun event, but it's not something I can do right now'

'Can I get back to you on that?' (which is always better than saying 'yes' when you mean 'no'!)

'I won't be able to make it that evening, but do have fun and give Sam my best'

If a colleague asks you to take over some of their work and you already have enough on your plate:

'I really wish I could, but truthfully now is not a good time'

'It's just not possible for me this month'

Never over-explain or be tempted to insert a long-winded, clearly fabricated story. Less really is more! Develop this habit by starting with situations that aren't quite so emotionally taxing; for example, with a colleague before you target your mother! It's true that the more you do it the better at it you'll become.

STAGE THREE – BE CONSISTENT

What next? Well, in a sense the hardest part has happened but, and this is crucial, if you've set a boundary you must be fully committed and remain consistent with your request. Do not give in and think, *'I'll let it go this one last time'*. Stay firm no matter how guilty you feel. It's imperative that you honour the original commitment you made to yourself. Remind yourself of why this is so important to you. If you don't stand your ground, you're negating all your hard work and dismissing your own request. You are telling the universe that you don't deserve this new behaviour. In truth, this is where most people stumble. They are met with a negative reaction and they jump in with a *'never mind me, it's fine really!'* making things a thousand times worse and leaving you feeling a million times more miserable. Don't let that be you!

There's a strong chance that you could be introducing boundaries into a relationship that has thrived on having none.

So be patient and just don't expect instant results. It rarely happens that way.

Those who won't want you to introduce boundaries will be the very people who benefited from you not having any in the first place

Expect to be challenged, expect pushback and expect fear. When you notice any of these responses, revert immediately back to why you want this, why it matters and why you decided to do it in the first place. Remind yourself that this was always likely to happen but that the reason you're doing it (your motivation) remains the same. Expect resistance and you won't be surprised or disappointed.

Try, if possible, to understand why the other person acts the way they do, not so that you can excuse them but so that you can see their behaviour as being separate from them and to your relationship. When you have a much better sense as to what might be causing them to react a certain way, it really helps you to depersonalise it.

It won't land perfectly in every situation. It may well be met with acceptance and rejection in equal measure. But the process itself teaches you so much, not just about yourself but also about how you are perceived by others. You learn who's willing to do what's needed and who isn't.

I only knew acceptance when I accepted myself
I only knew protection when I protected myself
I only knew support when I supported myself
I only knew love when I learned to love myself
We teach others how to love us, by how we love ourselves.

THOUGHTFUL TOOLS

- Where do you feel the most resentment in your relationships?
- Where do you feel your boundaries are being constantly crossed?
- Who repeatedly treats you in a way you know is no longer acceptable or tolerable?
- What's your biggest fear when it comes to communicating your desire for better boundaries?
- Where are you afraid to do what you want? And why?
- How will you feel when the boundary has been put in place?

CHAPTER 13

YOUR DAILY PRACTICE

The most successful people who achieve what they desire in life all have one thing in common: a consistent daily routine or practice. I do know that including the word 'daily' can be incredibly off-putting, as you think *'please, dear god, no, not something else I need to do'*, but try to focus on the benefits of consistency and find one that feels right for you, something you know you'll enjoy doing.

You're always in search of new ideas, new ways of doing things, and yet you completely overlook the fact that for you to be able to receive anything new you must first create space for it to land. A daily practice is one sure-fire way of achieving this, with the aim being to facilitate organising the contents of your mind better, reduce the chaos and create plenty more space for new thoughts, ideas and opportunities to drop in.

NO MORE EXCUSES

Daily practices can feel like another hurdle to cross, especially if you are resisting change. If, however, you're open to the idea of feeling differently, then you will be much more amenable to *doing* something different. Trust that the millions of people who regularly cite the benefits of implementing at least one daily practice can't all be wrong. But also know that if you don't change, nothing changes.

We all know the excuses. 'I just don't have the time', 'I'm already so tired', 'I'll wait until… and then I'll do it' or 'as soon as this happens, I'll start then'. All excuses. All rubbish. You either want to feel differently or you don't.

I'm going to go out on a limb here and guess that the worst part as you read this is knowing that I'm right, and appreciating that if you don't change things, you'll find yourself back in this exact same place, complaining about not being able to change. And who wants that? This has the potential to be a never-ending cycle until you disrupt it. Putting aside 15 minutes a day will disrupt it. So instead of asking, '*can I afford the time?*' let me throw it right back at you: can you honestly afford *not* to?

My non-negotiable practices

I've been known in the past to perform quite a distinctive eye roll at the mere mention of a daily practice. I recognise now that it wasn't because I was against any of these activities per se, I just didn't understand them. I didn't really know what they were referring to, nor did I know the first thing about what the real benefits of having a daily practice might be.

SO, WHAT IS A DAILY PRACTICE?

Before I regale you with the delights of my personal daily practice or routine, let's go back to the beginning and remind ourselves exactly what constitutes a daily practice and the real, tangible benefits of committing to showing up for ourselves daily. Well, the truth is this. You need them. These aren't tools you use to make things appear better when you feel low; these are tools that will help you feel grounded, rooted and connected when you are living your everyday life. These things that you do that require discipline are the very tools that will help you develop your ability to effectively navigate life and all its twists and turns.

Rebecca Campbell in her life-changing book 'Light is the New Black', beautifully describes why this is so important when she says: 'You cannot hear the callings of your soul if you don't carve time out to listen to them with daily, non-negotiable spiritual practice.'

Examples of what you can do as part of your daily practice include some of the following. This list is not designed to be exhaustive (or scary), but I hope it might inspire you to explore some, even out of curiosity…

Journaling	Nature
Meditation	Breathwork
Movement	Visualisation
Intention Setting	Manifestation
Affirmations	Gratitude
Prayer	Cacao
Learning	Yoga/Pilates
Vision Board	Inspirational Podcasts/Audio Books
Arts & Crafts	Soul work

Before you keel over at the thought of having to work your way through this entire list, let me assure you that you would not, or could not, be expected to do *all* these things, but hopefully one or two might appeal to you. I've done each of these (and plenty more) at some point in the last decade whilst on my own healing adventure. Some I loved and continue to do to this day, but some I didn't resonate with and knew that, at that time, they weren't for me.

Don't tell anyone, but you're my favourite

I'm going to talk here about several activities and will make references to the benefits of each, but the ones I will focus most on are my own personal favourites; the three I consistently show up for each day, which are: Journaling, Nature and Prayer.

There are days that I will spend the first hour of my day on these and yes, of course, there are also times I'll be very lucky to grab even fifteen minutes. You can make it work no matter what time frame is available to you. **But be aware that the days you really don't feel in the mood are exactly the days you need to show up the most!** The important thing is to keep turning up.

I also recommend varying each practice every few months in order to maintain the momentum and avoid finding it becoming too repetitive.

Prayer for me might mean reading books on spirituality, investing my time in exploring soul work, having internal conversations as I go about my day, or it might consist of a 10-minute meditation or even recording three points of gratitude. Nature might involve getting out amongst the trees every morning, planting my bare feet on the grass and participating in an earthing and grounding exercise, sitting in silence by the ocean, or taking my laptop out into the garden. While Journaling could feature me producing pages and pages of freestyle writing each morning or it might be answering one question each day in four short bullet points.

There needs to be flexibility in what you're doing. You want consistency but you don't want mind-numbing repetition. Knowing the difference *makes* the difference.

Journaling

I'm a big fan. Can't hide it, won't hide it. I think everyone should be encouraged to journal every single day. It's the Marie Kondo for the mind. Unquestionably, it's the most effective way I know for decluttering the brain. After more than forty years of consistent journaling, I love that I still get surprised by what comes out each day on that page in front of me. I've journaled, yes, you've guessed it, since I was six years of age!

Another plus for me with this daily practice is that you don't have to worry about saying the wrong thing, upsetting anyone or offending everyone. In addition, because the thoughts go directly from your head to the page, it gives way to a level of honesty that no other form of communication can give you. You don't need to engage a filter and it will always be the one place in your life where you will feel free to be yourself.

When you journal, you'll also be able to observe a pattern of what keeps coming up for you. Although, you may not want (or be able) to read what you've written. I rarely read back over my journals; instead, I love to perform a ritual burning ceremony every six months and watch all those thoughts go back out into the universe!

Journaling requires no financial investment apart from having your pen, paper and just 15 minutes of your mornings. Once you have two to three weeks under your belt, I promise you'll really start to notice the difference as increased clarity starts to creep in. But know this, there is no right or wrong way to journal. Think about what you want to articulate at that exact moment and write that. Start where you are. Always approach your journaling with a curious mind and a very open heart!

I hear from so many within my community that the hardest part for them is knowing what to write and that's why I created this Journaling Guide full of prompts that will give you a kickstart. Simply go to www.niamhennis.com/journaling and you'll find a long list of prompts that'll inspire you to take out your journal and write. You have no excuses for not getting stuck in now!

Nature

Four years ago, we moved across the country from the suburbs of Dublin to live within five minutes of the most beautiful woods in the West of Ireland. I know now that Dad led me here, but it was the woods that pulled us here. They saved me. I didn't know I needed them until I had them. As soon as it is light, I'm there, every single morning. Me, my dog Bella, and the trees. It's the most calming and reassuring part of my day.

I even have my very own favourite tree. It's actually not the prettiest one, or even the healthiest one. It's perched on a mound separate from all the other trees around it, but I felt pulled to it the very first time I walked past it.

My multitasking skills are in full flow as in those forty

minutes I can tick off movement, intention setting, tree-hugging, stone-touching, grounding, affirmations, gratitude and not forgetting the dog-walk! Getting out into nature, feeling such a part of it, getting that fresh air into my lungs and connecting with the earth is my non-negotiable start to the day. But it's a richly rewarding one also.

When you feel a little stuck in your head, moving your body into nature even briefly can really shift the energy inside of you. It doesn't require going into a forest or walking by an ocean; just getting out of your own space and into the great outdoors will do it. It could be going to your local park or even stepping out into your back garden. Rediscovering an appreciation of nature can be one of the most surprising and thrilling parts of your own reconnection process.

Prayer

My faith had always meant so much to me growing up and it was always a big part of who I was, but now, faced with so much upheaval in my life, I just didn't know where it fit in or where I belonged anymore. I really struggled for years with this. I wasn't at all sure how I was going to reconcile my need for connection to something bigger than myself with all that had happened. Being religious and being spiritual are two very different things and consequently, you do not need to be religious to pray.

I do not believe that prayer means sitting in a church reciting learned verses to your god. Prayer for me is a conversation I have with the highest version of myself. I think of who I am speaking to as my creator, source, energy, the universe, light, and even the trees. Whatever language resonates best with you to enable you to do this is the one you should think of.

Speak to them, talk to them just like you would to a friend. Your understanding of who this might be to you will change and evolve. You will question, challenge and rely on them. You need them. We all do. I can pray now because I always feel heard. Not because every prayer gets answered but because every prayer gets listened to.

Prayer helps us to feel heard and less alone. Some of you may have a very strong attachment to your creators and some of you may even possess a blind faith. But from my own heart, I ask you to think about what prayer means to you. When you need help, who is it you turn to and who is it you feel like speaking to the most when you feel alone?

That's who I want you to pray to. Every day I have a chat, I pray. I give thanks, I praise, I question, I challenge, and I check in the same as I do with my friends or family. Using affirmations, reading, writing, singing, music, meditation, walking outdoors; no two days of prayer are ever the same. It's different for everyone, but you have to figure out what it means to you. You must allow the space for those questions to be answered.

Prayer is how you communicate with the universe; it's how you make yourself known and heard in the infinity that is space. Prayer can be your channel of communication – the direct line between your soul and *your* creator.

The three practices above are examples of what you can implement to form your daily routine. If you're considering exploring these then I'd really encourage you to start small. Pick one activity from the list above that appeals to you and carve out a piece of time each morning to try it. Don't hide behind the excuse of *'not having enough time'* or *'not being able'* to do something on your own. You can and you will if you really want to. If it means setting your alarm clock twenty minutes earlier so that you can journal for fifteen minutes, put your focus on what the benefits might be and do it. This isn't about giving yourself something extra to do; this is about putting greater order back into your life. It's about creating space and making you a priority in your own life. It will ultimately help prepare you to make better decisions and with more ease. Remember, the answers you seek never come when the mind is busy; they come when the mind is still.

SOME ADDITIONAL POTENTIAL PRACTICES TO CONSIDER

Breathwork

This refers to any type of breathing exercise or technique. Many people report that breathwork promotes deep relaxation and leaves them feeling energised. They perform it to improve their mental, physical, and even spiritual well-being.

How you breathe contributes hugely to how you live. When you work at it and master your breathing, you feel alive, full of energy and relaxed. Breathwork gives you something to focus on as you're gently guided through each breathing exercise and is a powerful way to keep you calm in stressful situations. At its most basic, it slows you down and really makes you feel like you are exhaling all that doesn't serve you and inhaling what will make you feel better.

Grounding

I don't feel that 'being out' in nature is simply enough. Getting fresh air, being by the sea, in the countryside, up a mountain, in the forest or in the park are all more wonderful ways to introduce you to the heartbeat of the world. Observing the changes as each season slides in and out can teach you everything you need to know about your own life.

Connecting to nature and grounding in nature is such an immediate way to learn how to connect to yourself. When your bare feet hit the grass, or you feel the soft roughness of clay beneath you, you know in that moment what it is to be part of it and for it to be part of you.

When next you do this, picture or visualise the negative energy leaving your body through your feet and falling through the earth. Then call back in calming energy and feel it rising through the earth into your feet and back up through your body. You are not separate from nature but a part of it. Nature is who you are. It was here before you, it is here with you now and if you protect it, as is your responsibility to do so, it will be here long after you.

Reading

I used to think that in order to get the most from your reading you should only read one book at a time. I'm happy to report that these days I have three or four on the go at any given time. Whatever kind of book challenges you to think about being bigger and better, or when you find a writer who feels like they are speaking directly to you, keep them close. Analysing new beliefs, appraising new ways of thinking and acquiring new information all serves to inspire you and expand your imagination.

Audiobooks/podcasts

I'm a traditionalist when it comes to books. There is no

substitute for physically feeling a book in your hands that you can underline and make notes on. But I also enjoy listening to an audio of my most loved books (*after I've read them physically*) on long journeys. Podcasts are also excellent for this. Again, find material that will continue to stretch or inform you! Shameless plug alert: if you haven't already, take me on a car journey with you by tuning in to my **Tough-Love Energy** podcast available on all good platforms!

Early morning riser

I'm sorry. I really am. I know you probably had really hoped to get to the end of this chapter and not see any mention of crazy early-morning starts, but during the months of April through to October I really like to be at my desk at silly o'clock in the morning. I honestly recommend it as a way of really reconnecting with the world around you. It's by far the best time of the day to do your journaling, reading and prayer; free from all interruptions and distractions right before your mind starts filling back up. And you get to feel smug for the rest of the day too! Much of this book was written at the unearthly hours of 5-7am, mid-summer while watching impressive daily sunrises and a gorgeous herd of cows from my window!

Your environment

What can limit some people from introducing a daily practice into their routine is a lack of space. Please don't think that you need a separate room where you can go and do your journaling or meditating. You absolutely don't. If you can, take over a corner of the bedroom or a windowsill and place a beautiful candle, photograph or statue there that comforts you. If you have your favourite essential oils, incense or crystals, a plant or some flowers, place them here also. This will become your special place once you fill it with things that conjure up beautiful memories.

Rituals

Being Irish, I feel very proud that so many beautiful spiritual traditions started here in our country. Believe it or not, Halloween (or Samhain) originated in ancient Ireland and is a Gaelic festival marking the end of the harvest season and the beginning of winter, or the 'darker half' of the year. In the Wheel of the Year, eight festivals are celebrated, four of which have Celtic origins and are known by their Celtic names: Imbolc, Beltane, Lughnasadh and Samhain.

These along with the New and Full Moons (occurring every alternative fortnight), the Winter and Summer Solstices, our birthdays, and the welcoming of the calendar New Year all give you an excellent opportunity to check in on your life, to see where you are at, to set new intentions, release what's not serving you and feel part of a global community of people who are doing the same.

MEDITATION – FROM PAIN TO POWER

To encourage you to get started on your daily practice, I have written and recorded this very special meditation just for you. This nourishing 12-minute recording will tenderly guide you through the steps of releasing your pain and calling in your power.

www.niamhennis.com/meditation

THOUGHTFUL TOOLS

- What has been stopping you from taking the step to doing something new and are you ready now to prioritise yourself?

- What one new daily activity would you like to introduce, and will introduce, into your life for the next three weeks?

CHAPTER 14

RECONNECTED

Let me start by saying: congratulations, you made it! You've arrived on the other side. It may be the first step on the other side, but you are finally on your way and are already so much better equipped to set off on the next part of your next adventure. Step by step, you've done what has been asked of you. You are starting to feel reconnected again. You feel it because you are. You sense the flow that has been reactivated once again between your head and your heart. This is how alignment feels. This is how you move on from the past and step into the future, however uncertain that might be. This is how you learn to trust yourself and the energy of the universe.

Just as everything you dream of being you already are, everything you dream of doing you already do. When you reconnect with yourself, you reignite the light inside of you; you shine bright again from within. You become radiant again.

Choose now exactly where are you going to put your focus

201

and who you are going to let narrate this next part of your story. Are you going to continue to hand that power over to others, so that they can tell you what they think is an acceptable way for you to live your life, or are you going to choose that for yourself?

Let your life be bigger, bolder and more colourful than you ever imagined it could be. Don't be limited by the stories you've lived, but imagine the stories up ahead that you truly desire for you and create them.

Be led by your soul. What is it telling you it wants? What feels most in alignment and what feels right for you for where you are now? It's always about what feels right. Ask for help. Pray.

The joy you feel now at being fully connected again needs to be shared. The world needs to hear what your message is. It won't always feel easy or comfortable sharing it. You will question why anyone would want to hear what you have to say. You'll imagine what others will think when they witness you expressing it. But none of that is your concern. Remember, your mess is your message and by sharing it with others, as I have throughout this book, you will give someone else the gift of feeling heard.

Your task and your purpose are to shine your light, to share your joy, to radiate and release your message, whether that be your art, your music or your writings – whatever you know your gift to be is what must be shared. This is not the downside of being reconnected, rather this is the proof that you are.

You've done the hard bit.

You've given yourself permission.

You have detached yourself from the drama and self-pity.

You are free from your past; it no longer defines you.

You have moved from pain to power.

Freedom isn't the power to do what you want. It's the motivation to do whatever it is you want.

MY INVITATION TO YOU

I ask you now to let go of all you have ever known and all you have ever lived, then create the space needed to receive all that you have ever dared to dream was possible for you. It is here you will find peace. It is here you will recognise the beauty of simplicity as you reconnect with your inner self and the world around you. You are done listening to the noise. You're no longer avoiding what's coming because you believe that what is calling to you is something you are calling in.

You have faced the difficulties and challenges that life put in your path. You faced them, but most importantly you have navigated them. I am incredibly proud of you for having come this far. You are showing yourself that this is indeed your time to shine.

So much will shift for you once you start to make your life simpler. As your world and all that is in it shrinks, you grow. You expand into all that empty space that you have now created. That space which once might have terrified you is now where you will feel confident to grow and thrive.

Until you stop caring how it will look to others – how it will come across, how people will react – and until you see that your happiness is inside you, listening to your own voice, your soul's voice, nothing will change. When we resist change, we reject living. It's when we decide to take back control and to make the necessary changes that the lightness can begin to reappear in our lives.

There's a timing and an intention, to it all. Your hurt, your losses, your tears and your pain will feature in every story, but do you want them to be the only part you remember when you place the book of your life down at the end? Detaching from your drama and choosing not to let your past dictate your future could be the very thing that liberates you.

There is no success or failure, no right or wrong way of doing any of this. All I ask is that you observe your thoughts, your feelings, your actions and your behaviours. Check-in often and see what's coming up for you.

Keep gently edging your way forward, away from the drama and the stories. You are now accepting what life has thrown at you. You have integrated it into who you are and have also chosen not to let it determine who you become. You are so very capable and you are strong. You have the power to be who it is you want to be.

Believe that.

Trust that.

Trust you.

THOUGHTFUL TOOLS

Now you are reconnected again, take one last look in the rear-view mirror and answer these questions. Record your answers so that they may serve as red flags if they were to re-appear in your life sometime later.

- Where were you hiding and where were you not being true to yourself?
- Where in your life were you dismissing the whispers of your soul?
- Where were you being distracted by the thoughts and opinions of others?
- Where can you now live more simply and know that it will mean you will live more authentically?
- How can you immerse yourself more in nature?

A REMEMBERING

Sometimes you must disconnect from it all just so that you can learn how to reconnect with the deepest parts of yourself - Unknown.

EPILOGUE

Home is wherever you are. When you reconnect to yourself, a rebirth occurs. Those parts that were blocking you fall away and in their place, the next version of you – the better version – appears and blooms. You are no longer spending your time chasing the dream, trying to be better or to do better because you are now simply focusing on living it and being it. You are no longer attached to your drama because you are free to be now who it is you want to be. You are no longer afraid to go inward because you know it is there; you grow, it is there you get to start again. It is there you feel most powerful.

All transformation is about learning, observing, testing, changing, starting over and growing. Each stage brings you closer to where you think you should be and where you feel you want to be.

I've carried a deep knowing, which I now know to be a belief, that we each have a calling. It is not a pre-determined fate about which you have no say; it's your purpose and your reason for being here. The part of you where this lives is your soul. It's the part of you that makes you feel connected to life, to your source.

Your mind thinks of them, your heart feels them, but your soul is them

Every gentle nudge, inkling, whisper and sign comes from that place deep inside of you. When you feel drawn to people, places or happenings, it is your soul steering you there. Mostly, it speaks to you in inaudible ways, but if you continue to ignore it repeatedly it will inevitably make its presence known.

In my lifetime, I have missed so many of the signs when they were sent to me. I was distracted and, on those occasions, I thought I heard them, I didn't trust myself enough to trust them. But somewhere deep in my soul, I felt sure that my purpose was to inspire and activate change in others.

While I was busy ignoring the signs, I yearned for dramatic life experiences that I imagined would qualify me to inspire others through my words. I had none, but I lived in hope. Can you see how crazy that was? I silenced my voice purely because I didn't feel I had suffered enough to speak of suffering to others.

If ever there was proof that my manifestation game is strong, there it is. I asked for dramatic life experiences (yes, plural) – and they came in multiples. One after another. Loss after loss. Death after death. Until I was literally the last one standing.

If I was looking for evidence, I got it.

If I was looking for dramatic life experiences, I had them too.

When I was ready to heal, had processed and integrated the losses and was done wallowing in my own self-pity, I began to feel and hear that calling again.

'I want to inspire people. I want someone to look at me and say because of you, I didn't give up'

This is who I always wanted to be. But to get there, I knew I needed to move away from pity and detach myself from the drama that had unfolded in my life. The truth is, without the pain and the loss that I experienced, I would never have had the courage to do what I'm doing now. I would never have felt confident enough to ask people to make changes in their life without having to make so many in mine.

As I accepted this, I felt myself release the attachment to all that was bad in my life and begin to refocus my attention on all that could and would be good. It's that same nudge that literally extracted me from the city I called home and, albeit temporarily, replanted me back among the trees in the West of Ireland, just so that I could heal as I rediscovered and reconnected with who it is I am already becoming. This is what happens when you listen to the whispers of your soul. I am so glad I did.

When you write directly from your heart and your soul, you not only illuminate the road ahead for your readers, but you provide illumination for yourself too

So, what then is my calling? Well, I believe I've lived this exact life in order for me to be encouraged to write about and share these life experiences so that you might feel less alone. I believe my calling is to show you that when you're truly ready, you can make changes that will impact your future, despite anything that has happened in your past.

For as long as I can remember, I have wanted to inspire transformation, big and small, and always at the deepest level possible. It's why I now do what I do and it is why my unique coaching style works for so many. Guiding others now through their change and transformation, showing them that they won't have to do it alone, building their confidence, ensuring they feel heard, pushing them forward, holding them accountable, saying '*I understand what you're going through*' and honestly meaning it. Because I do.

I firmly believe that when you look back you can always see the breadcrumbs that took you from there to here. You might not always be aware of it, especially when you are living through it, but with some distance, you get the chance to see what you might have first missed.

I also believe that not everything that happens to you has to be good for it to be important. Whatever has happened to you, whatever setback you experienced, inside it contains learning and a suggestion as to what to do next.

What's in a name? A lot, as it happens

Throughout all of this, it felt like the answer was in my name. It was calling me to do more. In stepping up and shedding who I was, I started to see that for me to shine brightly, the answer was located in me stepping right back to who I was in the very beginning. Niamh (Irish pronunciation: derived from Old Irish Niaṁ) is an Irish feminine given name (meaning "bright" or "radiant"), which was originally a term for a goddess.

In Irish mythology, she who bore it was Niamh of the Golden Hair, daughter of the sea god who falls in love with

Finn's son, Oisín, and takes him to Tír na nÓg (the land of the young), where they stayed for three hundred years.

Well, this golden-haired goddess is ready now.

I am no longer the girl who bad things happen to

I am the woman who has experienced difficult things. In and of themselves they were not unique or unusual; what was different was that they happened in a condensed period of time. In sharing them and how I navigated my way back to myself, my sole aim is that I might inspire and help others to transform their lives also.

I know now for sure that all the things I share and everything I teach, even the things that don't always feel so comfortable, are exactly the lessons that I once needed to learn the most. Too many of us are reluctant to say *'I'm stuck and nervous to ask for help'*. I'm hoping this book will change that for you and help you feel less alone with your struggles.

You were never meant to do this business of life alone. Ram Dass described it so beautifully, and perfectly, when he said: *'We are all just walking each other home.'* And so, dear reader, I want to thank you for the honour of allowing me to walk with you on this important part of your journey.

Throughout these pages, we will all have observed one thing: that healing and transformation is a process. There is a beginning and a middle, yet the end remains charmingly elusive. The key is not to stay stuck in the beginning and not to let the middle become our ending. The thrill really is in the chase.

I'm deeply grateful that you chose to read this book to the end. I'm deeply touched that you let me share my story with you and I am deeply honoured that you allowed me to be part of your own transformation.

The beginning of your story now starts with the ending of this one.

-THE END-

ABOUT THE AUTHOR

Niamh Sheeran Ennis is a leading Change & Transformation Coach, who through her private practice, writings, programmes, workshops and podcast has inspired and helped thousands of people to make significant changes in their lives. She is an accredited *Personal, Leadership & Executive Coach* and a weekly contributor to www.IMAGE.ie; her work has also featured in The Business Post, Irish Country Magazine, The Irish Independent and The Irish Times.

WEBSITE: www.niamhennis.com
INSTAGRAM: @1niamhennis
FACEBOOK: @niamhenniscoach

FREE RESOURCES JUST FOR YOU!

I have created some great free resources just for you on my website, which I add to regularly.

You can find out how to create your own affirmations, receive a PDF containing journaling prompts, download a Bespoke Guided Meditation or listen to all of the episodes on my Tough Love Energy Podcast:
https://www.niamhennis.com/get-unstuck-resources

WANT TO GO DEEPER?

'RESET FOR CHANGE' 1:1 COACHING PROGRAMME

In this 12-week one-to-one private coaching programme, I ensure you feel fully supported and heard. I'm right beside you, guiding you, steering you, listening to you, working with you, challenging you and providing you with all the tools you are going to need to make and maintain these changes. I hold you accountable every step of the way and will never tell you what you want to hear, but always what you need to hear. This is where my Tough-Love Energy lives! That's why it's my most popular programme. To join the waiting list, just click here:
https://www.niamhennis.com/reset-for-change

THE CHANGE ACCELERATOR PROGRAMME

This self-study programme inspires and guides you towards that transformation you've wanted but didn't feel ready for, until now. That new career, those new boundaries, your finances and improving your relationship with money, working on your self-belief and worth and feeling aligned and purposeful while doing it all – if you are ready for them, and

I'm guessing you are, then stop talking and start doing!

https://www.niamhennis.com/accelerator

TOUGH LOVE ENERGY PODCAST

The podcast where I share with you the tools you need to transform that part of your life that you know is making you miserable. Working through a variety of topics, you'll leave each podcast feeling like you've had your very own 1:1 coaching session with me along with the practical next steps required to keep the momentum going! Be prepared to hear not what you want, but always what you need! https://www.niamhennis.com/podcast

THE CHANGING ROOM

Join our beautiful group of like-minded souls who are each preparing to make changes in their lives: www.facebook.com/groups/thechangingroom1. I've some fun plans for this Free Group, so it's a great time to come on board.

THE CHANGE NEWSLETTER

Receive free gifts, notes and exclusive updates from Niamh by signing up for her newsletter on www.niamhennis.com/signup

STAY CONNECTED
Website: www.niamhennis.com
Facebook: NiamhEnnisCoach
Instagram: @1niamhennis
Twitter: @NiamhEnnisCoach